# Managing People and Projects in Museums

### ABOUT THE SERIES
The American Association for State and Local History Book Series addresses issues critical to the field of state and local history through interpretive, intellectual, scholarly, and educational texts. To submit a proposal or manuscript to the series, please request proposal guidelines from AASLH headquarters: AASLH Editorial Board, 2021 21st Ave. South, Suite 320, Nashville, Tennessee 37212. Telephone: (615) 320-3203. Website: www.aaslh.org.

### ABOUT THE ORGANIZATION
The American Association for State and Local History (AASLH) is a national history membership association headquartered in Nashville, Tennessee. AASLH provides leadership and support for its members who preserve and interpret state and local history in order to make the past more meaningful to all Americans. AASLH members are leaders in preserving, researching, and interpreting traces of the American past to connect the people, thoughts, and events of yesterday with the creative memories and abiding concerns of people, communities, and our nation today. In addition to sponsorship of this book series, AASLH publishes *History News* magazine, a newsletter, technical leaflets and reports, and other materials; confers prizes and awards in recognition of outstanding achievement in the field; supports a broad education program and other activities designed to help members work more effectively; and advocates on behalf of the discipline of history. To join AASLH, go to www.aaslh.org or contact Membership Services, AASLH, 2021 21st Ave. South, Suite 320, Nashville, TN 37212.

# Managing People and Projects in Museums

## Strategies that Work

MARTHA MORRIS

ROWMAN & LITTLEFIELD
Lanham • Boulder • New York • London

Published by Rowman & Littlefield
A wholly owned subsidiary of The Rowman & Littlefield Publishing Group, Inc.
4501 Forbes Boulevard, Suite 200, Lanham, Maryland 20706
www.rowman.com

Unit A, Whitacre Mews, 26–34 Stannary Street, London SE11 4AB

British Library Cataloguing in Publication Information Available

**Library of Congress Cataloging-in-Publication Data**

978-1-4422-7365-8 (cloth)
978-1-4422-7366-5 (paper)
978-1-4422-7367-2 (electronic)

♾ ™ The paper used in this publication meets the minimum requirements of American
National Standard for Information Sciences—Permanence of Paper for Printed Library
Materials, ANSI/NISO Z39.48-1992.

Printed in the United States of America

# CONTENTS

CONTENTS

# LIST OF ILLUSTRATIONS

# PREFACE

The need for this book is obvious. The museum field requires strong management and leadership in order to maintain relevance and meet the challenges of a complex world. In particular, management systems that support the efficient implementation of projects and that respond to the needs of a productive workforce are often missing. The majority of work in museums today is project based. For example, collection moves, renovations, exhibitions, and public programs all require organization of resources (funding, time, space, and individual efforts). Project management systems are being used in many museums but sometimes fail due to the key component of human resource management. This text will outline best practices in managing people *and* projects in museums.

In the late 1980s and early 1990s I was part of a team of people at the Smithsonian's National Museum of American History that developed a formal project management program. My colleagues Ron Becker and Douglas Evelyn as senior managers believed in the importance of improving management of our exhibitions in particular. We continued to refine this program and established an Office of Project Management in the mid-1990s. Formal training of museum staff and the creation of project manager positions ensued. Today the museum continues to use project management systems, as do many other museums at the Smithsonian; and as my research reveals, it is used in museums across the country and around the world.

In 1993 at the request of Marie Malaro, program director of Museum Studies at George Washington University, I began teaching a class titled Managing People and Managing Projects. This class was designed to combine practical disciplined management concepts and the all-important understanding of the role of people in the success of organizations. Much of what this class covers is drawn from my MBA studies and ongoing learning about organizational development. From both my own professional role in managing projects in a large and complex organization and in my efforts to benchmark the best practices in the field, I have brought case studies to the classroom. The project management class continues to be an important offering in the GW Museum Studies program. After twenty-four years of teaching this class, it was a natural step for me to codify these lessons for museum professionals, both emerging and seasoned.

I hope this text will serve many audiences, including museum and nonprofit governing boards, executive directors, department heads, and staff, as well as consultants who work for museums and volunteers and interns. The book will also serve as a much-needed textbook for museum and library studies degree training programs. Both the American Association for State and Local History and the Institute of Museum and Library Services have hosted programs to train individuals in project management.

In this book readers will discover a practical guide to managing projects and important lessons about the role of individuals in the workplace and their critical role in the success of organizations. Throughout the text I address both business management theory and museum practice. The chapters are illustrated with the experiences of museum professionals as well as literature from the field and beyond. Specifically, the book covers organizational behavior theory; the critical overarching step of strategic planning, staffing, and human resource development; and leadership's key role. Contemporary leadership challenges and needed skills are covered as well as the link to ethical decision making. Chapters on selecting and managing projects, policies, and processes are included along with cautions on dealing with inevitable pitfalls. Decision systems are a critical factor in assuring that projects meet the needs of the organization. The mechanics of planning a project, including feasibility studies, chartering, establishing timelines, and assigning roles, along with developing budgets, is covered. Several management issues that are common pitfalls in museum projects are highlighted. A substantial part of the text examines the formation of high-performing teams with an emphasis on understanding individual differences and communications. Particular emphasis on the process of managing teams and dealing with conflict along with a focus on the importance of an effective project manager is covered. The final chapters of the book include evaluation of success and a set of nine case studies from a variety of types and sizes of museums. These case studies cover exhibitions and outreach, museum construction, and applications in small- to medium-sized museums. The Appendices include helpful project decision templates, charters, and other management tools used by museums today. Two hypothetical class exercises are also included for the reader to test their expertise in solving project management dilemmas.

I would like to thank the many people who helped to bring this book to life. First my gratitude to Dr. Kym Rice, assistant director of the Corcoran School of Arts and Design at GW, for encouraging me to take on this project and many other professional endeavors, and assuring I have had time to develop and share these lessons. Thanks also to my colleagues at the Smithsonian, including Harold Closter, Spencer Crew, Dennis Dickinson, Nanci Edwards, Patrick Ladden, Kate Fleming, Lauren Telchin-Katz, and many others over the years who have believed in the importance of project management. I thank also Bob Beatty and Cherie Cook of the AASLH and Dr. Steven Hoskins, who have created and offered a workshop series on this topic for many years. Also to Mary Case, Greg Stevens, Wendy Luke, Marsha Semmel, L. Carole Wharton, and Walter Crimm, who brought their good ideas to the classroom. Many fine examples of best practices illustrated in the book come from practitioners in the field, including Lisa Craig Brisson, Robert Burns, Cinnamon Catlin-Legutko, Peggy Day, Cathy Frankel, Rick Hardin, Trevor Jones, Elaine Harkins, Allyn Lord, Steven Miller, Jessica Palmieri, Laura Phillips, Josh Sarver, Christa Stabler, Kelly Tomajko, Daniel Tuss, and Stephanie Shapiro.

Finally, I thank my editor, Charles Harmon, for his guidance and encouragement during the writing and editing of the text. A special word of thanks goes to my husband, Joe Shannon, who is a consummate team builder and project leader and also has been consistently patient in supporting my research, teaching, and writing.

# INTRODUCTION

T he museum field requires strong management and leadership in order to maintain relevance and meet the challenges of a complex world. In particular we need management systems that support the efficient implementation of projects and that respond to the needs of a productive workforce. The majority of work in museums today is project based. For example, collections moves, renovations, exhibitions and public programs, or artifact digitization all require organization of resources (funding, time, space, and individual efforts). Although project management systems are being used in many museums today, they often fail due to the key component of human resource management. This book will outline the best practices in managing people and projects in museums.

## The Museum Context Today

The expectations and challenges of the nonprofit sector, including museums, are daunting. Headlines frequently illuminate financial struggles, closures, mergers, leadership turnover, or public controversy over programs. As widely admired as museums are, they face challenges of funding, audience relevance, and staff motivation. Nonprofits have big challenges: they lack the discipline of the bottom line, they struggle with accountability, they have a complex set of stakeholders, and their ability to solve problems is confounded by the ambiguity of expectations and often a lack of measurable data.

In response to the need for improved management and leadership in museums and nonprofits, there exist many educational programs designed to shore up the sector. Top universities such as Harvard and Stanford provide extensive degree programs and continuing education training for nonprofits. Other organizations such as National Arts Strategies and BoardSource offer a variety of training options to build leadership capacity. National museum organizations such as the American Alliance of

Museums (AAM) and the American Association for State and Local History (AASLH) provide options for training in management and business-related skills. Museum studies programs are increasingly adding management and leadership courses to their degree programs, while business schools have offered arts and nonprofit management programs. Even art schools are now focused on the intersection of the social sector, innovation, and the creative economy.[1]

Despite many options for training, museums have suffered a number of management problems over the years involving financial mismanagement, legal and ethical collections management failures, governance neglect, and poor leadership, as we can see from these examples:

- Governance missteps at the Smithsonian Institution and the Getty Foundation included excessive pay and benefits, conflict of interest, and lack of accountability that led to increased public scrutiny and sanctions to tighten management systems.[2]

- Collections were put at risk due to aggressive deaccession and sale at museums such as the Corcoran Gallery of Art, New York's National Academy of Design, and the Delaware Art Museum.[3]

- Museum expansion programs are very expensive investments that reduce funds available for staffing and other core programs. Despite billions of dollars invested in museum renovation, expansions, and new buildings since the mid-1990s, studies suggest an overinvestment in projects that have no clear demand. Unfortunately the risks associated with these projects can lead to closure, layoffs, long-term financial strains, and mergers.[4]

- Economic recessions are a fact of life in our world, and as they cycle in and out the impact on museums can be considerable as endowments shrink and philanthropy recedes. Government funding of arts and culture is directly related to tax revenues as well as political policies, as was evident from the 2015 to 2016 shutdown of the Illinois State Museum.[5] The federal deficit and global competition has also impacted funds available for the National Endowments, Institute of Museum and Library Services, and National Science Foundation. In addition to this the change in the US administration also could threaten the viability of these important arts and humanities funding programs. As museums react to these financial strains and economic impacts they must make hard choices about filling staff positions, promotions, and reducing funds for core programs. The impacts on the museum workforce are significant.

## Why Project Management?

Most of the work of museums is project based. Unfortunately we hear frequent complaints about projects that are taking too long, costing more, and making our staff miserable. Project management systems have been successfully used for decades in the manufacturing, service, construction, and government sectors. Starting in the mid-twentieth century this technique was applied in military, aerospace, and manufacturing settings, closely followed by use in the growing information technology and management consulting world. A disciplined and organized approach to work is standard in these sectors. While museums have been managing projects for decades, their systems can vary widely with inconsistent standards and poor results. This book will look at how to survive the process and optimize project outcomes and the role of staff in this endeavor.

Project management is defined as a set of activities that require dedicated resources to deliver a strategic goal within a defined budget and timeline. Around this definition are hundreds of theories, practices, tools, and structures. Indeed the Project Management Institute was founded in 1969 to provide professional certification, networking, research, and defined standards to a group of global practitioners numbering close to three million.[6]

The museum project management process ideally begins with a decision matrix that assesses feasibility: the risks and rewards associated with a given project, such as an exhibition. Once approved by management (e.g., the museum executive director or governing body), a project is chartered. For example, an exhibition charter specifies a theme or topic, team of staff (and possibly outside consultants), an assigned space, collections, a target opening date, and a working budget. A project manager is assigned to coordinate the detailed planning and implementation, including milestone reviews, team member deliverables, and a set of evaluation metrics. A substantial part of this book will explore the elements of project management for a variety of types of museums and projects. Important focus will be placed on decision making for projects in an organization, the need for flexibility in reaching goals, and the various ways that innovation plays a part in a modern museum. Topics such as self-managed teams, agile planning, design thinking, and rapid prototyping will be examined. At the center of these theories and systems lies a focus on the individual in the organization. Our staff needs to be armed with the skills to be successful.

## Why Managing People?

The good news is that mission-driven organizations such as museums have a strong sense of ethics and empathy that attracts committed staff and volunteers. The bad news is that people make programs succeed or fail. Museums need to treat their staff with respect and provide opportunities to excel in their work. The following are the types of internal organizational challenges that can occur particularly in a time of change, as discussed above:

- With reduced resources museums need to find ways to do work more efficiently, yet redesigning work processes or reassigning work due to a reorganization is painful for many. Although technology can help streamline work, it may also change the nature of the worker's role and status.

- How do we plan for demographic changes in the workforce? For example, the workforce is composed of many aging workers and challenged by a lack of diversity.

- How can poor internal communications create problems and misunderstandings that impede progress?

- How do we keep overworked, stressed staff satisfied and motivated?

- Could organizational changes create internal dissent and staff turnover?

- Could the individual quest for personal power and recognition ambush production of an important exhibition or other program?

## People Management Theory

Historically there have been two main threads in management thinking in regard to people in the workplace: the "scientific" approach focused on processes, incentives, and productivity, and the "behavioral" approach focused on individual psychology and motivation. Both of these strands are important to managing people. The writings of Frederick Taylor and Henry Gantt were influential in the development of scientific management in the early twentieth century when manufacturing was predominant. These individuals believed in the need for work incentives and pay based on outputs, time standards, improvement in procedures, and efficiency. Scheduling and production via diagrams were in common use.[7]

Perhaps in reaction to this thinking the field of workplace psychology espoused a more human-centered philosophy. The behavioral sciences looked at morale, motivation, and social relationships in the workplace. Important studies revealed that group dynamics and positive attention from management were directly correlated with productivity and self-esteem. Opportunity for growth in responsibility and autonomy were also positive factors.[8] These theories laid a foundation for the modern service-oriented workplace, which was described by Peter Drucker in his seminal works on management in the mid-twentieth century. The need for team-based work and flatter structures was a consistent theme in Drucker's writing. First to write about the "Knowledge Society," Drucker saw how the information age changed our work and how management specialists needed to work together in teams, with fewer layers of intervening hierarchy, calling for "smaller self-governing units."[9] Having written thirty-nine books as a consultant and professor, Drucker was an early champion of the value of nonprofits in society.

Other management and leadership theories have evolved in the past fifty years that focus on customer service (total quality management),

5

benchmarking best practices, innovation in organizational structure, systems thinking and learning, emotional intelligence, visionary leadership, and managing change in a volatile world. These theories are the basis of effective organizations in the modern age and will be discussed as they relate to the dynamics of successful project management.

This comprehensive text will cover the context for projects in examining several critical practices in organizational success. An in-depth review of the process of strategic planning will cover the steps involved in articulating the museum's mission and vision for the future, the major goals and objectives in implementing the vision, the resources and organization structures required, and the means of evaluating success. A focus on understanding the external environment and examining best practices via benchmarking similar organizations will be covered. In addition, a more flexible model for the contemporary museum world is that of strategic thinking. Examples of effective approaches in business and museum case studies will be illustrated. The text will also focus in on the importance of building an organization structure and resilient staff given the current workplace environment. The challenge of building a diverse workforce and accommodating expectations of emerging museum professionals will be reviewed. The importance of values and fair process along with staff development will be featured. Issues of staff voice including unions and other organized groups in the museum are discussed. A review of the literature on modern leadership theory as reflected in the writing of important thought leaders will also be examined in detail and linked to the practices of several model museum leaders. In conversations with various museum professionals there is consistent concern over a disconnect between leadership and the project manager. In fact, if leaders are not supportive of staff, including those who manage projects, then the systems will fail. In discussing these issues with colleagues in the museum field, there is a consistent call for top management support of project management systems and approaches. And once systems are defined and instituted there is need to be rigorous in employing them. Without this it is most difficult to achieve positive outcomes.

To focus on project management, the text covers the steps of launching a project, building the team, defining parameters and assumptions, developing budgets, and monitoring success. Extensive discussion of teambuilding, understanding differences in personality, managing communication, and dealing with conflict will be featured along with means of project evaluation and lessons learned. The text aims to provide views of practitioners in the field today, and these will be illustrated throughout the chapters. Finally, to provide a more in-depth analysis of the variety of ways that projects are managed in museums, a set of nine detailed case studies are included along with practical resources for individuals and organizations.

The text will draw on the author's experiences as well as that of today's museum professionals in applying project management techniques and principles. A variety of museums have contributed information to the development of this publication. This includes specific project case studies as well as documentation on decision making, project implementation, and evaluation systems.

## Discussion Questions

1. What problems do you see in how projects are developed and managed at your museum?
2. Consider how people-management concerns might impact the success for museums of various staff sizes. Do small museums need project management?
3. How do the scientific and behavioral theories of management relate to project success?

## Notes

1. The growth of nonprofit and museum management training includes the Getty Leadership Institute at Claremont College and the more experimental interdisciplinary degrees that combine art and business, such as the MA/MBA program at the Maryland Institute College of Art in Baltimore.

2. In 2007 Secretary Lawrence Small left the Smithsonian after revelations of funds mismanagement and conflict of interest. The Board of Regents was ordered by Congress to overhaul bylaws and make membership and decision practices be more accountable. The Getty Foundation president Barry Munitz was similarly ousted in 2006 due to excessive pay and other perks after an attorney general investigation.

3. Carolina A. Miranda, "Museums Behaving Badly: Are Sanctions Too Little, Too Late?" *Los Angeles Times*, June 21, 2014, accessed August 12, 2016, at http://www.latimes.com/entertainment/arts/miranda/la-et-cam-museums-behaving-20140619-column.html.

4. In 2010 the University of Chicago's Cultural Policy Center published *Set in Stone*, which covered survey data on new museum and performing arts building studies. Findings underscored the consistent overspending and struggles associated with sustaining these buildings after opening. For example, several museums have had financial struggles after building projects, including the Please Touch Museum, the Newseum, and Frost Museum of Science.

5. Tyler Davis, "Illinois State Museum to Reopen, Charge Admission," *Chicago Tribune*, June 28, 2016, accessed August 28, 2016, at http://www.chicago tribune.com/news/local/breaking/ct-illinois-state-museum-reopens-met-2-201 60628-story.html.

6. Project Management Institute, accessed August 6, 2016, at https://www.pmi.org.

7. Historical theory associated with human resource management includes seminal works by Frederick W. Taylor, *The Principles of Scientific Management* (New York: Harper and Brothers, 1911); Henry L. Gantt, *Organizing for Work* (New York: Harcourt Brace, 1919); and Peter Drucker, *The Practice of Management* (New York: HarperCollins, 1956).

8. In the early twentieth century several theories were developed around industrial psychology, including the work of Abraham Maslow, "A Theory of Human Motivation," *Psychological Review* 50, no. 4 (1943): 370–96, which focused on the hierarchy of needs and workers' quest for self-actualization. Writing in 1933, Elton Mayo's ideas about group work and motivation were chronicled in *The Human Problems of an Industrial Civilization* (New York: Macmillan Company, 1933).

9. Peter Drucker, "The Coming of the New Organization," *Harvard Business Review*, January–February 1988, 51.

# THE BIG PICTURE

## Strategic Planning and Organizational Development

No matter what type of project you are launching, the museum must do so in the context of an overarching strategic plan. Indeed, planning is the best predictor of success for any organization. Fortunately, museums today are well aware of this imperative. Very few funders will consider a request if the museum has not completed a strong strategic plan. There are many other types of plans that will be produced by your museum, including collecting plans, facilities master plans, education and interpretive plans, business and operational plans, and plans that support the functions of marketing, staffing, communications, and fund-raising. This chapter will focus on the process of developing an overarching strategic plan and provide examples of successful planning approaches in museums.

## The Strategic Planning Process

The process of strategic planning involves many players, intensive data gathering, decision making, and the strong commitment of museum leadership. The plan is typically meant to improve performance, lay groundwork for major projects such as an expansion, respond to changes in the environment, or secure AAM accreditation.[1] Preparing for planning requires a dedicated team of board and staff, communication systems, and identification of key information sources. The planning team must schedule regular meetings and document their decisions in writing. Sharing the work of the team on a common server accessible to all involved is recommended. Typically a staff member is selected to oversee the process, provide access to needed information, and maintain a record of the planning work. Working with outside consultants to facilitate the process can be very helpful as it does give museum board and staff the ability to focus more on the content of planning. Key players in the planning process include members of the governing board (who have fiduciary duties), the CEO or executive director, staff and volunteers, and community and advisory groups. Outside expertise will be needed during the process. For example, if your museum plan includes a major building program, you will definitely need advice from architects and engineers, exhibition designers, as well as state or local government officials and various funding bodies. The time involved in completing a strategic plan can be anywhere from a few months to over a year. Understanding the time commitment is critical, as is assuring that planning is a high-enough priority that day-to-day operations do not impede the efforts.

The process of planning requires the understanding of your organization's existing legal charter, mission, and its history in the community. These are fundamentals that will influence your decision making as planning proceeds. The phases of planning start with an environmental analysis and move through establishing the museum's mission and vision, setting broad goals and specific objectives, assessing needed resources, implementation of projects, and evaluation of success in meeting the mission (see figure 2.1). These phases are circular and sequential so that evaluation of success and lessons learned feeds back into the environmental analysis phase.

Environmental analysis is also known as a SWOT analysis, in which the museum gathers data on its strengths, weaknesses, opportunities, and threats. Expect to spend a significant amount on time on this phase of planning as the museum will need to do a good deal of research. See figure 2.2 for an example of the types of information that should be collected. *Internal factors* will require gathering information about collections, exhibitions, educational programs, facilities, staff, finances, membership and fund-raising, and technology. Assessing strengths and weaknesses, for example, could include the fact that despite having a first-class collection it is not accessible to the public due to limited space or lack of online availability.

The data-gathering effort can be done by staff and board members or outside consultants. For example, assessing the strengths of exhibitions should be the responsibility of staff curators, educators, designers, and collections managers, while assessing the facilities could require outside

**Figure 2.1. Strategic planning process. Courtesy of the author.**

engineering or security experts. Members of the museum's community should also be invited to participate in the process, sharing expectations and observations on the museum's relevance. Many museums take advantage of assessment programs funded by the Institute of Museum and Library Services, National Endowments for the Arts and Humanities, and AAM's Museum Assessment Programs. The leadership of these efforts can be assigned to key staff or small task forces. Other consultations involve examining the issue of organizational culture and values, an honest look at staff morale, and community perceptions of the museum.

*External factors* may take more effort to catalog, as understanding the

| **INTERNAL FACTORS** | **EXTERNAL FACTORS** |
|---|---|
| • Collections<br>• Staff<br>• Facilities<br>• Culture and Values<br>• Reputation<br>• Finances<br>• Programs | • Economy<br>• Location<br>• Demographics<br>• Cultural Trends<br>• Political Factors<br>• Competition<br>• Legal Constraints |

Figure 2.2. SWOT analysis. Courtesy of the author.

market for your museum programs will certainly require extensive visitor evaluation studies. Investigating the current and future trends in technology, tourism, education, demographics, and globalization can be daunting. Drawing on the data of major studies such as the American Alliance of Museums's TrendsWatch reports or the Horizons report of the New Media Consortium are two helpful examples.[2] This phase of planning requires an assessment of legal constraints that might affect hiring, collections acquisition, access for disabled visitors, and IRS reporting requirements. Also of critical importance are the standards and best practices of the museum field, including AAM's Core Documents and continuously evolving ethical guidelines. Particularly important to project management are matters associated with workforce changes, including demographics, fair labor practices, diversity, work-life balance, and professional development.

Other external factors requiring examination include geographic location, building codes, physical structure and square footage, and neighborhood characteristics, public transportation, and other access concerns. Equally important is your competition. Imagine being one of nineteen Smithsonian museums on the Mall in Washington, DC. How do you compete for audiences? Aside from other museums, there are many competitors for the attention and time of the public (e.g., sports arenas, theaters, parks, libraries, or other educational programs). And certainly all museums must consider the enormous draw of the Internet and networked devices.

Finally, you need to consider the impact of public policy in support of the arts, sciences, and humanities and the interests of private funders (both individual and foundations) that will be strategically important to the viability of the museum. Foundations have varying priorities depending on the economy and societal concerns. Government funding for the arts has diminished considerably over the past thirty years, and there are continuing concerns about the nonprofit sector's tax exemption status. Increasing emphasis on the museum as a driver of economic development and community growth as well as a significant player in workforce development is an important external issue.

*Benchmarking* or examining the best practices of similar museums is another key tool in the SWOT process. Elizabeth Merritt, writing in *Secrets of Institutional Planning*, recommends that museum staff and board become familiar with plans of similar organizations.[3] What makes those organizations successful? During an extensive planning effort at the National Museum of American History in the 1990s, staff interviewed and visited many museums looking at a number of practices including interpretive planning, organizational structure, advisory boards, facilities expansions, and capital campaigns. Their findings were useful to confirm thinking about visitor focus, collections storage, organizational change, and capital campaign management.[4]

Assessing the large array of SWOT data collected will require time to digest, and it is wise to share this information widely with all staff and key stakeholders. A process that was used at the National Museum of American History in the mid-1990s involved the formation of sixteen task forces composed of self-selected staff teams that completed the SWOT process and presented findings and recommendation to the entire staff over a period of several months. Lord and Markert warn that this phase can be difficult as weaknesses and criticisms can be difficult to accept. Being open-minded is important to a realistic assessment of the museum's situation.[5]

After digesting the information collected in the SWOT phase, the museum needs to invest its time and efforts in developing goals and objectives that will help it achieve its core mission. Understanding the community needs, areas for internal improvement, targets for growth of programs, and adopting new approaches to delivering transformative experiences will provide a clear direction for the future.

*Mission statements* need to be closely reviewed during strategic planning. In many cases the original mission may no longer reflect the goals of a museum that needs to remain relevant in the community. Older statements may be more of a laundry list of activities that the museum has been engaged in rather than a succinct statement of aspiration. The mission is your fundamental purpose and how it builds on strengths, impacts decisions, and motivates staff, board, and funders. Gail Anderson's seminal work on museum mission statements recommends that it is possible that the mission can change over time as the environment demands. A museum needs to create a statement that is short and sweet, choosing wording that will describe three elements:

- What is your purpose?

- Who do you serve?

- How do you deliver your services?[6]

Commenting on the importance of mission to nonprofits, Peter Drucker notes that a mission will succeed if it reflects the opportunity to serve a need, uses the strengths of the organization, and demonstrates a commitment on the part of staff and board.[7]

Like many museums, the Henry Ford Museum and Portland (Oregon) Art Museum both took the step of revising existing mission statements as a result of strategic planning efforts (see textbox 2.1). These statements are short, carefully worded, and clear in regard to the impact that they intend to make. Their assets are being directed toward programming that will clearly make an impact on their community and audiences. They use compelling words such as *authentic*, *diverse*, and *inspire* to predict that they will impact future generations.

*Vision statements* are closely related to the museum mission. Although there are various formats being used by museums today, the more successful vision statement is one that allows the museum to elaborate on a description of a successful future state. In most cases this will be a vision that is a set of stretch goals to be achieved over several years. In today's world the time horizon is likely to be three to five years, although if there is a major building program involved that time frame should be a good deal longer, perhaps as much as ten to fifteen years. Your vision needs to

## 2.1. Museum Mission Statement Examples

The Henry Ford provides unique educational experiences based on authentic objects, stories, and lives from America's traditions of ingenuity, resourcefulness, and innovation. Our purpose is to inspire people to learn from these traditions to help shape a better future.

\* \* \* \* \* \* \* \* \* \* \* \* \* \* \* \* \* \* \* \* \* \* \* \* \* \* \* \* \* \* \* \* \* \* \* \* \*

The Portland Art Museum is dedicated to serving the public by providing access to art of enduring quality, by educating a diverse audience about art, and by collecting and preserving a wide range of art for the enrichment of present and future generations.

*Source:* The Henry Ford Museum and Portland Art Museum websites.

make a compelling difference and implies significant change from the status quo. The museum's CEO/director should be the key player in articulating the vision that describes an organization that is a dynamic, engaging resource providing a variety of learning experiences, and making a significant impact on the lives of audiences served. The entire board, staff, and community stakeholders should endorse this vision. Some museums determine to use a short statement of vision, while others delve into more description. Although there is no standard, it seems best that a museum not skimp on this phase of planning. It will impact the ability to achieve buy-in from staff and significant funding for critical projects.

An example of a vision statement that is descriptive of a positive future state is that developed by the National Museum of American History in its 2013 to 2018 Strategic Plan. Building on its mission, the museum has developed a vision that seeks to define the meaning of America as "an idea and an experiment that has reverberated through the centuries—grounded in freedom, possibility, and opportunity." The vision continues with "over the next decade we will use our unparalleled collections to tell an inclusive, respectful, and compassionate story of all the peoples in America. . . . We will tell stories of perseverance, triumph, and optimism with those of struggle." The museum aims to do this "together with the America people" to "make a difference in the life of the nation."[8] In crafting a vision statement, you need to be sure that staff and the board understand its implications and support its implementation.

*Values* statements are often included in the strategic planning process. These words and phrases should guide the operations of the museum. Values are customarily meant to serve as guides for internal decision making and reflect the organizational culture. For example, the Oakland Museum in California adopted the following values statements:[9]

> *Excellence*: We are committed to excellence and working at the highest standards of integrity and professionalism.
>
> *Community*: We believe everyone should feel welcome and part of our community, both within the Museum and with our visitors and neighbors.
>
> *Innovation*: We embrace innovation and calculated risk taking to achieve our mission.
>
> *Commitment*: Our work at the Museum demonstrates a sense of purpose and a shared accountability for the institution's success.

Values are unique to the museum and should be developed by the museum's staff to assure buy-in. They reinforce the mission and serve as guideposts for communications with the external world. We will further examine the importance of values in the chapter on staffing.

*Goals and objectives* provide the meat on the plan. In many ways they respond to the gaps that were evident in the SWOT analysis and answer obvious needs and opportunities. Examples of museum goals might include new areas of collecting, upgrades to storage, collections digitization, new programs to serve community youth, responding to the impact of social justice issues, expansion of educational programs and special events spaces, improving internal processes, long-term staff development, and revenue-producing programs. Essentially they respond to the question: What are the activities we need to accomplish in order to realize our vision? The most effective organization creates a wide-ranging set of goals and establishes realistic objectives to achieve them. Goals should revolve around programs, staffing, infrastructure, collections, and resources. Knowledgeable staff should be intensively engaged in developing a balanced and feasible set of programs. And goals should be achievable within the given time frame. Examples of broad goals established by the Samuel P. Harn Museum of Art at the University of Florida in its 2013 to 2018 Strategic Plan[10] included activities in support of:

- collaboration and partnerships

- relevant and engaging exhibitions

- a sense of belonging

- innovation though technology

Although goals are broad and ambitious, they require more specific strategies or action plans to define a road map. Examples of strategies might include a new area of collecting, a new interpretive plan, an expansion or renovation, or a new educational outreach program for underserved audiences. In this regard, the number of possible goals and actions can become overwhelming. A plan with fifty strategic objectives that must be implemented in one or two years while undergoing a staff reduction is totally unrealistic. Unfortunately, we want to do everything because we have many great ideas. This phase of the planning process is most painful. After dreaming of many worthy new projects, we must make hard choices. This can be the downfall of many a strategic plan. The process of deciding becomes paramount here. How can we maximize the impact and effectively use the resources available? One way to approach this in today's museum is a feasibility phase in which prototypes can be tested in collaboration with the public. This is particularly important if the strategies involve a new area of activity for the museum.

*Resources* such as staff time, space, collections, and funding should be considered in tandem with the development of the strategic plan and not as an afterthought. Budgeting is a constantly iterative process as new information is added to the plans for new objectives.[11] Ultimately the budget will inform the fund-raising strategy of any needed capital campaigns. Typically in this phase museums need to develop business or operational plans that address several questions. What existing funds are

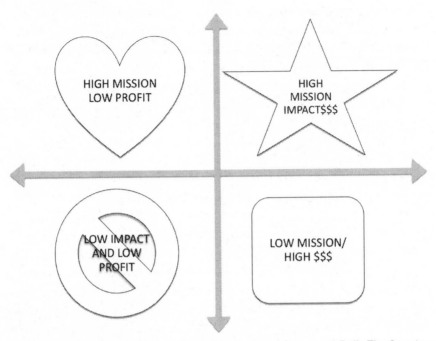

**Figure 2.3. The matrix map. Adapted from Zimmerman and Bell, *The Sustainability Mindset*. 2014**

available to seed or fully support these strategic objectives? Are funders ready to step up to launch these projects? Is there a future revenue stream available? What are the options for federal, state, and local grants, and corporate, foundation, or individual donations?

Other approaches involve a full analysis of the impact and costs of any new initiative. The use of feasibility studies is a smart step in assuring that we are capable of achieving our goals. This process can be very detailed in the case of a major initiative such as a new building, a new retail venture, or a merger or long-term partnership with another organization. Large and complex projects involve assessing fund-raising capacity, market surveys, detailed operational budgets, and skills analysis to secure needed expertise. No matter what the size of the endeavor, some level of feasibility should be developed in regard to staffing and other resources, impacts on existing programs, and funding goals. In most cases, looking at varied scenarios will also provide some guidance. Asking key questions about external impacts and potential failures will give the museum options to consider in determining a final green light for a strategic project. As noted above, given a long-term vision, the goals and objectives can be numerous. They should also be complementary. Improving the collections storage facilities should provide new opportunities for exhibitions and educational programs based on the collections. Diversifying the museum workforce should lead to attracting new audiences to the museum.

Nonprofit organizations working with constrained resources can benefit from a popular decision system called the Matrix Map (see figure 2.3). This approach allows an organization to make critical decisions about programs based on their impact and profitability.[12] Although nonprofits are not bottom-line organizations, the fact is that expenditures of funds, time, and talent can be assessed in regard to their impact on the museum's mission. Where an existing or new project lies in the four quadrants helps the museum determine its relevance. Perhaps funds can be reprogrammed from low-impact to high-impact areas to assure success. This approach requires a financial analysis of all programs, their success in audiences served or net revenue, and an impact analysis. Impact should at a minimum be defined as:

- relevance to mission

- responsiveness to audiences

- funding feasibility

- leveraging internal strengths and external partnerships

- adherence to legal and ethical mandates

Another consideration is that resourcing the plan frequently leads to a change in the organizational structure. Downsizing, creating new program areas, and reassigning staff leaders will change the way the organization operates. How does the museum need to operate, and what internal processes and communications structures are needed to achieve the plan's goals? For example, the Glenbow Museum created a new organizational structure as a result of strategic planning in the 1990s. The museum implemented a staff reduction and in the process developed a new mode of operation that was less hierarchical, called the Shamrock, consisting of

19

overlapping circles containing a variety of functional staff.[13] We will look more carefully at organizational structures in chapter 3 along with the importance of staff training and development.

*Implementation* of strategic goals relies on the use of project management. These systems create a set of activities that can be monitored over time, measuring progress along with budgetary expenses and the work of staff. In fact, no project should be launched without a careful assessment of its priority in regard to implementing the strategic plan vision. We will discuss this in greater detail in later chapters.

The *evaluation* phase of planning relies on a set of measures and outcomes associated with strategic goals. Measuring success is usually a matter of quantitative and qualitative assessments. For example, the museum might be using numbers of audiences served, funds raised, new collections acquired, and positive press reviews. Other numbers might include cost per square foot of renovated space, amount of turnover in staff, and changes in revenue models. More challenging is the qualitative analysis of short- and long-term impact in the community. Evaluation also requires a consistent approach over time involving defining a baseline of effectiveness and ways to measure change. The board, executive leadership, and staff need to be able to assess how well their plans have worked and where there are needed changes. This information will be part of the next SWOT analysis phase, thus completing the cycle as illustrated in figure 2.1.

Given the changing nature of our world, a strategic plan needs to be flexible. In fact, despite investing time and money in the process, there are still unexpected roadblocks that occur when key board or leadership leave the museum or funding simply does not materialize. Given these facts, we need to consistently review and update plans on a regular basis. In fact, new leadership, launching a capital campaign, or recovering from a funding crisis are all times when plans should be revisited and revised. David La Piana, writing in *The Nonprofit Strategy Revolution*, states that "traditional strategic plans, once complete, are not fluid and organic but static—and they quickly grow stale."[14] He calls for a "real-time" approach that allows for rapid response to a changing world. Traditional strategic planning is often plagued by unreliable data, delay and inaction, and resulting staff frustration. La Piana recommends that having the right people involved before planning and applying a decision system called a

Strategy Screen helps.[15] Much like the Matrix Map system discussed earlier, a Strategy Screen allows the organization to set decision criteria in the process of selecting key programs to fund. This is essential to assure flexibility in a changing environment. La Piana recommends decision criteria that consider mission, economic feasibility (does it pay for itself?), competition, and finally, the institutional capacity to succeed. An example of the usage of a Strategy Screen in museums is the Nebraska State Historical Society. Director and CEO Trevor Jones notes that this allows the museum to test the viability of an idea based on its service to mission, funding source, or partnership with other organizations. This is being used in conjunction with their strategic planning (see table 2.1).

## Strategic Thinking and the Context for Change

What is strategic thinking? It is how we respond to change in the environment, retain viability through delivering value to our audiences, and sustain our organizations over time. Strategic thinkers are engaged with understanding the big picture, applying innovative approaches, building financial viability, and measuring progress.

Today's museums are facing the following realities:

- *volunteer leadership* (the board)
- a wide circle of *stakeholders*
- a need to reflect *diversity* of audiences/demographics
- a lot of *competition*
- a *building boom* of new and expanding museums
- constant change in *technology*
- *limited resources* frequently mismanaged
- increasing reliance on *commercial endeavors* and corporate support
- *collections at risk*
- *employees are highly motivated* but are overwhelmed with work

**Table 2.1.  NSHS Strategy Screen**

The task/program/project or function under discussion:

| Criteria | Answer: ( +, − ) | Comments: |
|---|---|---|
| Is it consistent with our mission? | | |
| Does it build on or reinforce our competitive advantages?<br>1. Our statewide mandate<br>2. Our collections | | |
| Does it have a dedicated funding source and/or will it break even or produce a surplus within a year? | | |
| Does it help build or strengthen a partnership with another organization? | | |
| Does it help grow a target audience? (*draft audiences*):<br>• Local history organizations/ museums<br>• Students (middle school)<br>• Teachers<br>• Researchers<br>• State & local elected officials (advocacy)<br>• NSHS members/donors | | |
| Does it build on or support the work of other NSHS teams? | | |

Should we do it? _____

*Source*: Courtesy of Nebraska State Historical Society.

- *legal obligations* of public trust and accountability

- professional *standards and ethics*

Although strategic planning systems are still critical in this volatile and complex world, we need to put relevance and accountability at the forefront of our planning. In studies involving a variety of museums (twenty-nine respondents) conducted between 1995 and 2000, the following practices were identified in responding to a changing world:[16]

- increasing use of strategic planning
- new organizational structures, including cross-functional teams
- more frequent reliance on bottom-up communication
- an emphasis on improved organizational learning
- increased focus on customer service
- developing systems of performance metrics
- a link between strategic planning and growth in fund-raising and marketing

These findings revealed the growing practice of planning and its link to internal organizational change as well as a growing concern for working with audiences consistent with the call to action in the AAM's 1992 publication on *Excellence an Equity*, which emphasized diversity and community engagement. Since then the field has placed community relevance at the heart of planning. For example, the Canadian Museum of Nature developed a new model of "national service," creating a series of national research and collecting partnerships.[17]

Museum thought leaders have focused on strategic thinking and its deep understanding of audiences. John Falk and Beverly Sheppard have written about audiences as the museum's customers and the need for customization of experiences. Marketing theory can be used by museums to understand social and generational demographics, class distinctions, and learning style variances.[18] Another question is that of volatility in the environment. How can the museum respond to constant changes in society? John Durel has written about a model for sustainability that includes the following core elements:[19]

*Reputation*: strengthening your reputation through measuring impact

*Love*: building community and funder support based on deep commitment to customer service

*Prime:* building an organization that is strong and growing with a staff and board committed to entrepreneurial activities and professional development

*Money*: creating a diverse and balanced funding base

As we consider the practice of strategic thinking, museums today are refining their mission statements to increase impact in the community, provide love, and secure their reputation. Durel writes that value-added service results from responsiveness to external realities augmented by strong internal capacity. Museums that are providing this type of service have redefined their core mission. For example, the Children's Museum of Pittsburgh "provides innovative museum experiences that inspire joy, creativity and curiosity," while the Minnesota History Center is "using the power of history to transform lives." The mission of California's Santa Cruz Museum of History and Art aims "to ignite shared experiences and unexpected connections."[20]

Social responsibility is a central strategy in the work of many museums. This philosophy has been articulated in the writings of respected museum thought leaders including Elaine Gurian and Robert Janes. In her writings, Gurian has called for a new civility, diversity, and inclusion, and museums as safe spaces.[21] Janes has championed missions based on social justice and environmental stewardship, a values-based organization with a collaborative staffing structure, a focus on creativity and risk taking, and a rejection of corporatism.[22] Our thought leaders serve as the conscience of modern museums pushing for new strategies and approaches in crafting strategic plans.

Several museums have produced strategic plans that are uniquely accountable and relevant. The Chicago History Museum under the leadership of Gary Thompson, for example, created a new approach to planning led by staff and community members. Values defined in this process included empathy, authenticity, discovery, and creativity. Their guiding principles included the power of history, a focus on the city of Chicago as their major asset, and the importance of collections. They also valued service to the public, understanding and meeting audience needs, and looking for external partners. As a staff-led effort, the education director chaired their planning committee. And the views of staff were not only sought but also published in the vision document.[23]

The planning process led by Brian Kennedy and staff at the Toledo Museum of Art beginning in 2010 resulted in an exemplary *vision* for several reasons. First, it acknowledged the power of collections to model the creative process. Second, it strived to reach new audiences, make an impact in the community, to be an operationally responsible organization, and use resources responsibly. The museum completed two strategic plans between 2010 and 2016. The first was meant to gather wide input and support from stakeholders in defining goals and objectives and to restructure the museum to implement the plan.[24] The second planning effort resulted in the new vision outlined in textbox 2.2.

In a similar vein, the San Diego Museum of Man under the leadership of Micah Parzan completed a comprehensive three-year plan in 2011. Pillars of this plan included: increased public engagement, collections stewardship, financial stability, and building leadership capacity. Unique to this plan is its refreshing openness and honesty in explaining the context and background of the museum's history, its forward-thinking

---

## 2.2.   Vision of the Toledo Museum of Art

**Audience Growth:** The number of our actual and virtual visitors will increase.

**Diversity:** Our on-site visitors will reflect the economic, social, cultural, and racial diversity of our region.

**Community Relevance:** We will be an integral member of our community and will be responsive to issues of community concern and importance, particularly as they relate to the arts.

**Art Collection:** We will achieve a consistently high level of quality.

**Professional Leadership:** Other organizations will look to us as a model of operational effectiveness, integrity, responsibility to mission, and successful application of innovative solutions to solve real problems.

**Operational Excellence:** Resources will meet organizational needs, be built to realize organizational aspirations, and be allocated to achieve the Museum's mission and vision.

*Source:* Toledo Museum of Art.

---

focus on values, and its transparency in sharing decision-making criteria with the public. Their "strategic toolkit" includes a matrix to evaluate visitor experience and assess programs as well as the values of the museum.[25] In 2015 the museum published its Master Plan for physical transformation with details of measurable outcomes and accountable staff. The museum supports an open and experimental atmosphere in stating, "Everyone is an idea person." One unique and bold goal in this plan is "world peace starts at home," whereby professional development and team dynamics are fundamental programs. There is also a focus on development of social spaces in the museum and exhibitions and programs on current issues of social justice.[26] This plan is clearly responsive to the needs of the community and its social context. Its reputation will be built on this awareness.

Under the leadership of Director Dana Friis-Hansen, the Grand Rapids Art Museum also designed a unique strategic plan that launched in 2014. A focus on human-centered design thinking permeates this plan. The museum was the first LEED certified art museum in the country when it opened its new facility in 2007. Their leadership in innovation is a core value. The strategic plan includes a stakeholder map that is a graphic of the numerous groups who work with the museum as partners, audiences, and supporters. Goals include building civic and cultural leadership skills among staff as well as understanding the principles of human-centered design in order to facilitate programming. It is also important for the staff and board to become thought leaders in the community.[27]

The Mattuck Museum of Art and History in Waterbury, Connecticut, developed their three-year strategic plan around goals of transformational change and community revitalization. The plan is comprehensive in its focus on programs, collections, finances, staff, and board. Each major goal area has a set of performance measures to assure accountability. Executive Director Robert Burns led this effort in collaboration with a team of board and staff. Two years into the plan the museum had achieved significant growth in endowment and clear plans for a building renovation to improve programmatic space. As goal areas are implemented, the museum has taken the time for honest reflection on the less impactful projects and adjusted priorities.[28]

In conclusion, it is clear that museums must take the time to create a viable and flexible strategic plan based on sound data, including the voices of many internal and external stakeholders, and with realistic operational systems to support their dreams.

## Discussion Questions

1. Has your museum conducted a SWOT analysis? What are the top three concerns revealed in this exercise?
2. What are the metrics necessary to an effective evaluation system for your museum? Consider both quantitative and qualitative measures.
3. Consider the life cycle of your museum and how you would need to plan to achieve or maintain the state of Prime for your museum, as defined by John Durel.

## Notes

1. Gail Lord and Kate Markert, *The Manual of Strategic Planning for Museums* (Lanham, MD: AltaMira Press, 2007), 1.

2. TrendsWatch produced by the AAM Center for the Future of Museums, accessed August 27, 2016, http://www.aam-us.org/resources/center-for-the-future-of-museums/projects-and-reports/trendswatch, and "Horizons Report," produced by the New Media Consortium, accessed August 27, 2016, http://www.nmc.org/publication/nmc-horizon-report-2016-museum-edition.

3. Elizabeth Merritt and Victoria Garvin, eds., *Secrets of Institutional Planning* (Washington, DC: AAM, 2007), 103.

4. Martha Morris et al., "Benchmarking Studies, 1995–2000." Unpublished Internal Reports of the National Museum of American History, Smithsonian Institution.

5. Lord and Markert, *The Manual of Strategic Planning for Museums*, 47.

6. Gail Anderson and Roxana Adams, eds., *Museum Mission Statements: Building a Distinct Identity* (Washington, DC: AAM, 1998), 25.

7. Peter Drucker, *Managing the Nonprofit Organization* (New York: HarperCollins, 1990), 3–8.

8. John Gray, "Looking Ahead," in *National Museum of American History Strategic Plan 2013–2018*, accessed August 23, 2016, http://www.nmah.si.edu.

9. "Values Statements," Oakland Museum, accessed on August 14, 2016, http://museumca.org/careers/omca-culture.

10. Samuel P. Harn Museum of Art, 2013–2018 Strategic Plan, accessed August 20, 2016, at http://www.harn.ufl.org.

11. Merritt and Garvin, *Secrets of Institutional Planning*, 51–58.

12. Steve Zimmerman and Jeanne Bell, "The Matrix Map: A Powerful Tool for Mission-Focused Nonprofits," *Nonprofit Quarterly* (April 2014), accessed August 20, 2016, at https://nonprofitquarterly.org/2014/04/01/the-matrix-map-a-powerful-tool-for-mission-focused-nonprofits/.

13. Robert Janes, *Museums and the Paradox of Change* (Calgary: University of Calgary Press, 1997), 43–65.

14. David La Piana, Preface to *The Nonprofit Strategy Revolution* (New York: Fieldstone Alliance, 2008), xiv.

15. La Piana, *The Nonprofit Strategy Revolution*, 15; and author conversation with Trevor Jones on November 16, 2016.

16. Morris et al., "Benchmarking Studies, 1995–2000."

17. Joanne DiCosimo, "One National Museum's Work to Develop a New Model of National Service: A Work in Progress," in *Looking Reality in the Eye: Museums and Social Responsibility*, eds. Robert Janes and Gerald Conaty (Calgary: University of Calgary Press, 2005), 59–70.

18. John Falk and Beverly Sheppard, *Thriving in the Knowledge Age* (Lanham, MD: AltaMira Press, 2006), 52–55.

19. John Durel, *Building a Sustainable Nonprofit Organization* (Washington, DC: AAM Press, 2010), 9–25.

20. Websites of Children's Museum of Pittsburgh (pittsburghkids.org), Minnesota History Center (mnhs.org), and Santa Cruz Museum of History and Art (santacruzmah.org), accessed August 20, 2016.

21. Elaine Gurian, "Intentional Civility," *Curator* 57, no. 4 (October 2014): 473–84.

22. Robert Janes, "The Mindful Museum," in *Curator* 53, no. 3 (July 2010): 325–38.

23. "Claiming Chicago: Shaping Our Future," Chicago History Museum, 2006, accessed August 21, 2016, http://www.chicagohistory.org/documents/home/aboutus/CHM-ClaimingChicagoClaimingOurFuture.pdf.

24. Amy Gilman, "Institutionalizing Innovation at the Toledo Museum of Art," in *Fundraising and Strategic Planning*, ed. Juilee Decker (Lanham, MD: Rowman & Littlefield, 2015), 103–10.

25. "San Diego Museum of Man 2012–2015 Strategic Plan: A Blueprint for Success," accessed August 27, 2016, http://www.museumofman.org.

26. "Master Plan Narrative 2015 San Diego Museum of Man," accessed August 27, 2016, at http://www. museumofman.org.

27. "Grand Rapids Art Museum Strategic Plan and Statement of Purpose, 2014," accessed August 27, 2016, http://www.artmuseumgr.org.

28. "Strategic Plan 2014," accessed August 27, 2016, at https://www.mat tatuckmuseum.org/mattatuckmuseum/MattatuckMuseumStrategicPlan_2014 –2017%20small_0.pdf; and author telephone conversation with Robert Burns, August 29, 2016.

## CHAPTER THREE
# MANAGING PEOPLE IN MUSEUMS

S uccessful projects depend on talented, dedicated, and motivated staff. This chapter provides an overview of the best practices in working with people in the museum, including the process of hiring staff, organizing their work, and assuring top performance. It also addresses twenty-first-century workplace skills, managing performance, protecting staff rights, and workplace ethics.

## Overview of the Twenty-First-Century Museum Workforce

The contemporary workforce in museums and nonprofits is fraught with difficult challenges, including low pay and lack of diversity, and yet we continue to attract dedicated individuals striving to make a significant contribution as employees, volunteers, and interns. As of 2011 the museum workforce numbered close to four hundred thousand individuals working in over thirty-five thousand museums. The majority of these individuals is white and holds a college degree. The number of minorities is quite small.[1] The need for diversifying our workforce is clear but not easily resolved. Also, the retirement of baby boomers is resulting in a brain drain, requiring younger staff to be ready for stepping up to new responsibilities. Thus, training is a big issue. Technology is rapidly forcing organizations to scramble to keep up with new applications, and this impacts hiring and staff training. Family-friendly policies such as the need to accommodate childcare or elder care call for more flexible work schedules. Commuting problems and environmental sustainability efforts favor telecommuting, but this impacts workflow, meetings, office coverage, and communications. Staff may no longer need to be in the workplace, but the lack of face-to-face interaction can be a deterrent to productivity, morale, and team success. The millennial generation is less likely to be loyal to a single employer, more apt to move on to increasingly more lucrative or satisfying work, and to seek better work-life balance than previous generations. Seeking this flexibility and autonomy, workers are more comfortable with part time or project work. Emerging professionals are frequently advocates for a living wage and paid internships, and at the same time they are worried about the growing threat of artificial intelligence and robotics.[2]

Generational differences in the workplace can be a challenge for both workers and leaders as expectations are not always in alignment. As revealed in a study by Lancaster and Stillman, the four generations in the workplace exhibit attitudes and expectations that can be at odds. Members of the oldest silent generation (born before 1940) are comfortable with hierarchy and top-down decision making while generation X (born between 1960 and 1980) and generation Y millenials (born between 1980 and 2000) are more comfortable with collaboration, consensus, and multiple means of communication. Generational differences also apply to career goals. While baby boomers (born 1940 to 1959) have a sense of building a clear path and a single professional goal, younger generations are more focused on building a suite of portable skills and expect to hold a variety of jobs. Thus the latter will be less inclined to commit to working in a single museum over time.[3]

Not only do we have differences in generations but also the nature of work in museums has shifted. John Durel writing in *History News* in summer 2002 discussed the growing core of independent museum professionals with specialties that allow for short-term project work. This growing population of former employees is appearing at the same time that museums are willing to outsource more and more functions.[4] In addition, we see museum leadership seeking as much flexibility as possible in their hiring practices. Part-time work, job sharing, use of volunteers and interns, and outsourcing are common modes of developing a more flexible workforce and reducing the overhead costs of permanent employees. This may create financial benefits for the bottom line but can severely disrupt the social contract between workers and managers and among the individual workers themselves.

Reacting to a new set of workforce concerns, the Museums Association of Great Britain has embarked on studies of diversity initiatives and of the best methods to assist the emerging museum professional. A positive-action training program was undertaken in the United Kingdom from 1998 to 2011. The effort placed both minority and disabled individuals in workplace traineeships. Findings in a follow-up study noted that a majority of trainees actually secured positions in museums, yet there was a significant percentage who had or planned to leave the field altogether.[5] The reason for this turnover may be due to economic issues. Writing about the issue of entry to the museum workforce, Maurice Davies noted that employers are able to hire highly qualified individuals at low wages, which in the business world would be a triumph, but for nonprofits and museums this is a difficult scenario. Entrants to the workforce are highly frustrated with the process of seeking jobs. Compounding the problem of few jobs and many qualified applicants, Davies found that many museums do not see the value of museum studies degrees. Finally, museums do a poor job of training new recruits or existing staff for growth. Resolving this dilemma requires more conscious efforts at trainee-level programs as well as closer collaboration with university museum studies programs, for example.[6]

Similarly, US museums are increasing emphasis on diversity and workforce readiness. The Andrew W. Mellon Foundation published its 2015 report on diversity in art museums, with findings that detailed the predominance of nonminorities in professional positions.[7] Another study conducted by the Association of Art Museum Directors (AAMD) revealed that despite a growing number of women in the profession, their pay was not equal to men in similar leadership positions.[8] In 2013 the AAMD began a partnership with the United Negro College Fund with support from the National Endowment for the Arts and various foundations to create art museum fellowships for undergraduates from historically black colleges.[9] Fortunately, in response to these findings the AAM made workforce diversity a pillar of their Strategic Plan (2016–2020).[10] Despite this emphasis, much work remains to be done to address this issue, including improving the opportunities for underserved populations to do internships, attend higher educational programs in museum training, and be mentored through their careers. Challenges also remain in establishing benchmarks for higher wages for museum staff, particularly at entry-level positions.

## Staffing the Museum

### Organizing Work

The framework for implementing the museum's mission, goals, and objectives is an organizational structure that provides for a division of labor and coordination of efforts.

The traditional organization chart graphically describes reporting relationships that reflect not only specializations but also power and decision-making authority. In figure 3.1, the hierarchical organization is composed of leaders (the board and director) who set strategy, approve policies and activities, and delegate authority. Department heads or middle managers coordinate with peers across the museum as well as maintain professional standards and supervise the work of subordinate staff specialists. Museums are organized to reflect program areas such as exhibitions, collections management, education, public programs, and curatorial research along with administrative functions such as finance, human resources, fund-raising, marketing, facilities, and technology. Depending on the size of the museum, these functions might be stand-alone departments or the combined responsibilities of a few people. In larger organizations, staff advisors do studies or provide technical advice to senior staff and the board but have no formal authority. Departmental staff and volunteers are located under the various program areas to which they report.

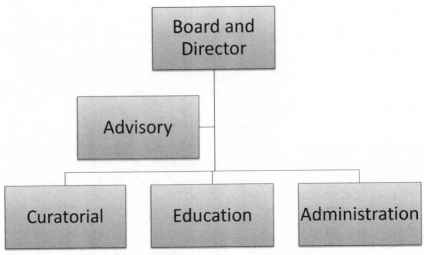

**Figure 3.1.   Hierarchical organization. Courtesy of the author.**

Generally the organization will operate under several principles, including unity of command where every person reports to one boss and the organization is divided by departments representing products or functions, while coordination of work occurs through shared resources and standardized policies and procedures. Despite the widespread use of the hierarchical model, there are alternatives. For example, a shamrock model in figure 3.2 consisting of overlapping circles reflects the reality of interdisciplinary collaboration on daily work in many museums. Another ad hoc model places emphasis on the external stakeholder's role, as is clear from figure 3.3.

Often the ad hoc approach is meant to emphasize the museum's mission and values more than draw a picture of formal reporting relationships. Overall, organization charts tend to change over time as the museum needs to add, eliminate, or combine functions. As a result of strategic planning there could be a need to add a new department (e.g., marketing, social media, technology) or combine functions that are similar, such as collections management and curatorial. In reality the charts are only a guideline since most staff will work through more informal networks at various levels of the organization.

Project management systems depend on a matrix organization concept. As teams are formed from the major departments of the museum, individual staff will work for a project manager as well as a functional

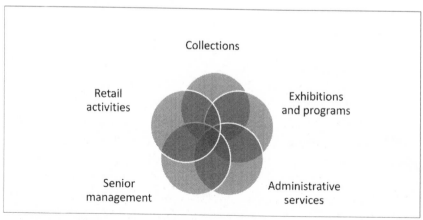

**Figure 3.2. Shamrock organization. Courtesy of the author.**

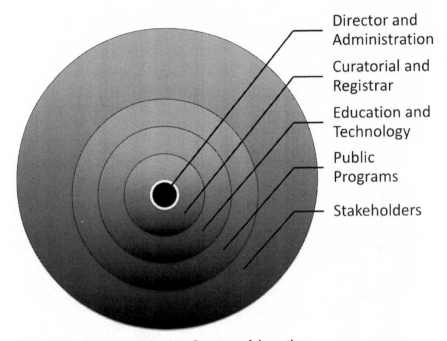

Director and
Administration

Curatorial and
Registrar

Education and
Technology

Public
Programs

Stakeholders

**Figure 3.3.  Ad hoc organization. Courtesy of the author.**

supervisor. Figure 3.4 shows an example of a project matrix chart where the functional offices assign key staff to work on project teams. For example, with an exhibition it is more efficient to create a team of curator, registrar, and educator to plan and implement projects collaboratively rather than in a separate and sequential manner. The team approach is advantageous as it enhances information sharing and problem solving. Teams are important because they allow for a mix of skills that includes people working together from different departments to complete a discrete project, such as a collection move or a special event. Depending on the overall schedule of projects, it is not unusual for staff to be assigned to work on several teams at one time. The unique issue for the team member is that they have two bosses—the functional manager and the project manager. This can create conflict and requires much communication and negotiation.

The value of the matrix and team approach is that there is more rapid development of a project, better understanding between units of the organization, and ability to be more responsive to changes. Creativity is

| Function/ Project | Curator | Education | Registrar |
|---|---|---|---|
| Special Exhibit | X | X | X |
| Collection Move | X | | X |
| Public Program | X | X | |

**Figure 3.4. Project matrix. Courtesy of the author.**

also enhanced. Similar to the team approach are short-term groupings such as task forces, standing committees, and advisory groups. These each will have a set of guidelines for their work and be subject to museum policies.

### Populating the Organization Chart

The work of contemporary organizations requires a set of skills that are unique. As outlined by the Institute of Museum and Library Services, the landscape of skills is wide ranging and diverse.[11] The list of skills for success in our world is daunting but has importance in building strong and sustainable museums. These skills are those that museums must rely on for success and will be important to museums as they recruit new staff. The skills include

- critical thinking and problem solving

- creativity and innovation

- communication and collaboration

- visual scientific and numerical literacy

- cross-disciplinary thinking

- flexibility and adaptability

- leadership and responsibility

Whether using volunteer or paid staff, the museum defines specific jobs that support the basic functions of the organization and its strategic goals. Clear roles and responsibilities are spelled out in written job descriptions and annual performance plans. Determining what staff the museum needs will depend on factors such as baseline functions, special projects, the budget, and operating policies. Museums also should have written policies that lay out the different types of work specialization, the pay levels and their qualifications and duties, and the opportunities for individual growth and promotion. Other policies will catalog the rights and responsibilities of employees and supervisors, codes of ethics, and workplace conduct.

A position description is the museum's contract with the employee and customarily will include:

- department assignment/title

- basic duties

- knowledge required

- supervision of others

- work location and physical demands

Recruiting to fill positions in the organization is a very important function to assure that the best-skilled workers are hired. Selecting the right person needs to be a thorough and thoughtful process. Recruitment involves describing and advertising the job, setting salaries, interviewing, and hiring the best candidate. Advertisements often describe work in great detail, and many times with extremely high expectations. It is important that the duties and qualifications be as realistic as possible. Museum staff does not "walk on water," and their job responsibilities should not be unachievable. Although the process of hiring is straightforward, there are frequently problems that can arise.

One of the first steps in hiring is to determine the type of work relationship that is best for the museum. The museum's strategic goals, existing staff, and budget will dictate whether work is to be permanent, temporary, contracted, or volunteer. If the museum wishes to contract

project work, there are considerations necessary to meet IRS requirements. The law requires that contractors provide a specific work product,
work with their own equipment, and work independently. Many museums today are outsourcing what were once core activities—exhibition
design, conservation, curatorial research, and cataloging along with more
administrative functions such as security and retail operations. Contract-
ing for services requires a formal process (the RFP), a staff coordinator or
project manager, and clear delineation of work products, timelines, and
payment schedules. Contractors do not receive benefits and must be personally responsible for taxes and insurance. Adding contractors to the
workplace can be stressful if expectations are not clearly defined.

Recruiting full- or part-time staff is the responsibility of department
managers and the museum's human resources staff, and most importantly
they must encourage a wide number of applicants, using a fair and legal
process of selection. No discrimination can be involved. Recruiting is subject to civil rights, disability, and age protection laws. All internal staff
should have the opportunity to apply if they are qualified. Jobs should
be widely advertised in a variety of places, including on the museum's
website.

Setting salaries is a critical part of recruiting. Benchmarking other
museums, reviewing the salary data in AAM or AAMD surveys, and
sharing information with other nonprofits or museums in the region are
all-important resources. Salary is only the baseline expense since the
museum must consider offering their full-time staff a number of benefits
including health insurance, life insurance, retirement contributions,
paid leave, flexible schedules, and other options such as training and
development.

The process of recruiting uses standardized applications that detail
specific experience, education, and other qualifications. Some positions
may have multiple applicants, and the museum must have policies in place
to govern the selection process. For example, the museum may determine
to interview only the top five or ten candidates from a large pool. The
interview process likewise should be the same for all candidates, unless
there are issues of distance in which a phone interview would be the best
option. For all interviews, a standard set of questions, the same team of
interviewers, and a similar amount of time devoted to the applicant is
customary. It is typical to have a team of interviewers meet the candidates

and to ask them to provide specific evidence that they are a match for the work culture. These teams are usually composed of a variety of managers or other staff, and sometimes can involve museum volunteers, board members, or other key stakeholders. More than one interview may be needed for the top two or three candidates to assure that as many stakeholders as possible get to weigh in on the selection. High-level jobs such as the CEO or director's position may involve an outside search firm to manage the process. References are critical to assure the selected candidate is going to be a good fit. There are other steps that might be taken in the selection process, including personality assessments or asking the applicant to solve a hypothetical workplace problem. Once the best candidate is selected and the decision documented, steps are taken to bring the new employee on board. As there may be potential issues with performance, a probationary period (often three to six months) will allow both the museum and new staff member time to adjust. If it doesn't work out, the person can be let go. This needs to be spelled out in the personnel policy of the museum.

## Orientation

Getting started in a job requires a formal approach to understanding the museum, its plans, its facilities, its finances, and policies. Not only should the staff member receive training for their specific job but also have a chance to meet all staff and board members. Informal gatherings are a great way to make a new employee feel comfortable. Beyond the position description and an individual performance plan, new staff should have access to the museum's strategic plan, budget and annual reports, policy documents, and organization chart.

Staff retention is important because the cost to replace and train new staff is high. Over 50 percent of a museum's budget can be dedicated to personnel costs. Investing in the long-term growth of employees is a wise approach. Beyond training in the skills and methods of the particular job, staff needs to stretch their knowledge. This may be done through special courses in new management systems or through attendance at a professional conference. Internal development programs that encourage skills via workshops, job sharing, and individual growth projects are important and often more economical. Mentorships can also make a huge impact on the growth of an individual no matter how experienced they are.

## Volunteers

Most museums are highly dependent on volunteer services for their survival. Individuals that have expertise and are committed to the museum mission can make significant contributions. Volunteers are most often motivated by altruism, the desire to meet new people and gain skills, and the feeling of pride in being part of an organization they love. Today's volunteers can do any number of jobs beyond the usual docent tour. From front desk reception to behind-the-scenes work with collections, volunteers need to have challenging work and feel valued by the organization. Many museums fail to develop a collaborative spirit among staff and volunteers that can potentially harm their relations with community members. For example, when new programs are implemented involving new work methods (interactive tours, new database systems), volunteers may be the last to be informed and prepared for change. The museum will need a volunteer policy manual that covers standards of conduct, ethics, and expectations on the job. Although they have many skills, volunteers should have limited levels of responsibility if there is any chance of legal liability. For example, a volunteer should not act on behalf of the museum in any legal negotiation such as gifts or loans of collections. In return for volunteer service, it is critical to include these individuals in special events, in the process of creating strategic plans, and other important programs. As with paid staff, respect and recognition of their service inspires volunteers to feel a sense of value. Interns also deserve similar coordination and direction, job descriptions, and evaluation of their work. Whenever possible, interns should be paid a stipend in recognition of their contributions to the work of the museum.

## Performance Management and Staff Development

Annual performance reviews are needed for all staff. Customarily they should be keyed to the museum's annual operational plans and special projects associated with the strategic plan. The supervisor will work with the employee on a set of goals for the performance period and enumerate ways to measure success. The standards of success may include numbers of projects completed, artifacts catalogued, deadlines met, or audiences served. The values of the organization should also be addressed, for example, the way that individuals behave in the team environment or the way that they will step up to challenges of developing innovative solutions to unexpected problems. Ways to exceed the basic standards will always be an issue. Employees are motivated to exceed the standard in order to achieve recognition or financial rewards. Measuring progress against goals should be done at frequent intervals (monthly or quarterly) where adjustments may be needed as circumstances may require midcourse changes. If there are problems, then perhaps more time, guidance, or training is needed. Consistent communications between supervisors and employees will assure there are no surprises.

Most importantly, recognition and rewards for performance are very important to ongoing retention and staff satisfaction. The following are possible ways to provide this:

- cash bonus

- time off

- a salary increase

- letter of praise

- public thanks

- service pins

For example, the National Museum of American History instituted a unique form of staff recognition in the 1990s. The Peer Awards program allowed staff to nominate individuals, departments, or teams of colleagues for exceptional work. A committee of staff members selected the award winners who were then honored at an annual all-staff and volunteer recognition program. Other ways to celebrate staff contributions could be annual staff picnics, all staff parties, frequent staff meetings, interactions with the board, and inclusion in openings or other membership events.

Along with the annual performance review, the staff should have opportunities for professional growth. Attending conferences, participating in webinars or workshops, specialized continuing education, or financial support for those staff seeking advanced degrees are examples. Other ideas include internal mentorships, opportunities for job rotation, and new projects. Surveys conducted in the late 1990s revealed that many museums invest minimally (less that 5 percent of total budgets) in this most important function.[12] Without this investment there are real risks for museums. In particular with the retirement of baby boomers and the expectation of millennials having several jobs during their careers, it is critical to provide training and development of existing staff. Grooming staff to move into senior positions is one need. Providing leadership skills at all levels assures that the organization will adapt to inevitable changes.

Despite careful hiring, orientation, and training, there is still potential for problems to occur with individual workers whether paid or volunteer. The museum's policies in regard to human resources management must reflect how problems are to be resolved. Importantly, a fair and clear process should be outlined to deal with employee problems. A system of progressive discipline from an informal discussion leading all the way to suspension or dismissal should be included in the official personnel policy of the museum. Workplace problems are usually either conduct or performance related. Conduct is defined as behavior that is disruptive to the museum's work or in any way threatening to other workers or the public. An example might be an employee who has angry confrontations with co-workers. Should a worker commit a crime (e.g., theft or assault), they will likely be terminated on the spot. Performance-related problems are typically mistakes or inability to complete work assignments. Remedies for either of these types of problems involve counseling, documentation, and possible dismissal if the problems are not resolved in a reasonable time frame. Each step of the progressive discipline approach should be clearly outlined for the employee, who should have the opportunity to respond and be represented either by an attorney or by a member of an employee union. In the case of performance-related problems, the individual can work with their supervisor on a performance improvement plan to correct problems. Employee counseling services should also be offered particularly if there are health issues. In the case of layoffs or furloughs related to financial decisions (instead of conduct or performance problems), a careful system of steps to final separation should include assistance in outplacement, a number of weeks or months of pay, and possibly continuation of health benefits to ease the individual's transition.

## Special Considerations of Museum Work

As Peter Drucker has noted, "One of the great strengths of a nonprofit organization is that people don't work for a living, they work for a cause."[13] Because the nonprofit workforce is subject to low pay and often long hours, there is an unwritten contract with management. I contend that there is a higher level of staff voice in the management of the organization as a result. This adds to the complexity of management-staff relations. Nonprofit workers also have a higher sense of ethics and workplace values, and for the most part they are proud of their work and their organization. The following problems are typical of nonprofits, including museums:[14]

- not enough people to do the work, not properly trained

- difficult to discipline poor performers

- need to reduce bureaucracy, improve communications

- high levels of stress

- few available jobs even for college graduates

- low pay, which exacerbates the reality of student debt

In regard to pay, recent efforts to provide a national living wage in Great Britain have been less than successful in their museum sector. This is due to the fact that museums have experienced funding cuts. Therefore, instead of raising wages museums add new duties to existing jobs or turn to volunteers and unpaid internships.[15]

In a similar vein, a series of staff surveys conducted at the Smithsonian Institution over the past ten years has revealed the following:

- limited promotion opportunities

- need for better internal communications and coordination

- a positive attitude about work

- concern about the openness to new ideas and creative endeavors

These studies give the Smithsonian management a snapshot of worker views and potential areas for improvement. For example, in 2008 shortly after the resignation of controversial secretary Lawrence Small, the level of satisfaction with senior management was only slightly higher than in previous years. In 2010 this had changed to more positive responses as transparency in decision making and a new institutional strategic plan was completed. The survey findings continued to highlight the lack of promotion potential along with new concerns in regard to cross-unit collaboration and work-life balance and diversity. By 2015 reports were showing greater satisfaction with these latter items but highlighted dissatisfaction with management's encouragement of innovative ideas and recognition and reward systems. The outcome of these surveys results in actions taken in management improvement plans.[16]

## Protecting Staff Rights

There are obvious concerns about the treatment of staff members in many organizations, and if pushed too far there can be significant push-back on part of staff. For example, the following scenarios discuss the issue of unions and other options for advancing worker's rights.

Staff marched outside the main entrance of the Washington, DC, museum carrying signs protesting unfair labor practices. These staff, which represented both professional and blue-collar ranks, shared common grievances. A newly appointed chief executive was making radical changes—eliminating programs and jobs, reorganizing the museum, centralizing decision making, and implementing controversial policies. Staff were distressed that an individual with a business background and no museum experience was appointed by the governing board to run the museum. The museum's director had essentially been relegated to the status of a middle manager. A national union was working with the most outspoken and militant individuals—members of the curatorial staff—to help them organize to fight this oppressive and unpopular new leader. The press quickly seized the opportunity to write embarrassing articles about the mistreatment of staff and poor management at the museum. Although this sounds very much a modern-day story, it actually occurred in 1971 at the Corcoran Gallery of Art in Washington, DC.[17] Another headline captured the public's attention about a year later. Gene Baro, director, and Vincent Melzac, CEO, exchanged punches at a public black-tie opening at the museum. At issue was the clash of styles, vision, and egos of an artistic director and a cost-cutting executive. They both resigned shortly thereafter.[18]

Moving forward to the twenty-first century, similar management challenges confronted Lawrence Small, who became secretary of the Smithsonian in 2000. Small was criticized for leading the museum into a new era of commercialism and corporate sponsorship, including inappropriate donor influence. Groups of scholars inside and outside the institution wrote letters of protest to the Board of Regents. Small was further criticized for proposed downsizing and elimination of what were regarded by these scholars to be important programmatic units and general disregard for the employees of the organization. Some of his actions even angered members of Congress. Newspapers and periodicals around the country and around the world ran numerous stories on this topic. The *Washington Post* quoted liberally from disgruntled curators and former directors—as many as six since Small began his tenure in January 2000.[19]

In early 2015 members of the United Auto Workers union at the Museum of Modern Art in New York picketed a black-tie reception at the museum. Museum staff carried signs criticizing the director and board for failing to provide acceptable healthcare benefits and cost-of-living raises. The union of professional and administrative staff did not go on strike as they had done in prior years. (Museum staff has been unionized since the 1970s.) The museum's management negotiated an acceptable settlement later that summer.[20] In 2015 another grassroots effort was born. A small group of museum staff and students from different parts of the country began to network via social media and face-to-face meetings over the issues of fair pay, unpaid internships and work-life balance, and issues of social justice and workforce diversity. Museum Workers Speak is a self-organized movement that has provided an important forum for workers and students to voice their concerns and advocate for change.[21]

### Workplace Ethics

All of these examples make it clear that there continues to be a need for fair treatment of individuals in the workplace. It is helpful to look at the larger picture examining what is going on outside museums in regard to how employees are treated and how they deal with organizational changes. Studies conducted in 1999 and 2000 by the Hudson Institute measured global employee loyalty and commitment in business, non-profit, and government. Surprisingly less than one-half of the employees who responded to the survey felt strongly committed, although a majority of respondents said they were proud of their organization. What most motivated people was fair treatment, followed by an atmosphere of care, concern, and trust. Organizations with published codes of conduct and operating values received the highest praise.[22]

A national study of corporate employee attitudes conducted in 2000 looked at the existence of codes of conduct or values statements, training regarding these codes, and enforcement of violations. The study showed a positive correlation between established ethics programs and modeling of values by leaders and supervisors with increased employee satisfaction, loyalty, and retention.[23] The latest reports of the Ethics Resource Center that poll employee attitudes about ethics note a rising number of incidents of misconduct on the part of senior managers who should be the ones to set the standard of behavior. Despite this rise in misconduct there is a rise in ethics training in the workplace, and overall fewer reported instances at all levels of the organizations responding.[24]

In reviewing the above examples both from museums and nonprofits, we see trends that concern fair treatment of staff. Ethical concerns are consistently on the minds of museum workers. Several areas tend to rise to the top of the list of complaints, including:

- conflict of interest

- employee mistreatment

- lack of adherence to professional practices

Conflict of interest arises when board and staff members make decisions that are self-serving as opposed to adhering to the mission of the organization. Excessive executive pay or other perks is one example. Another might be a donor with too much influence over programmatic decisions. Ignoring professional standards can occur in many ways but often it has to do with censorship in exhibitions or publications, or reckless deaccessioning, or ignoring collections preservation or workplace safety concerns. Another concern would be engaging in extensive for-profit revenue-generating activities that blur the lines and water down the mission. Employee mistreatment might involve poor communications of expectations, lack of sufficient resources for the work at hand, lack of voice in critical decisions, lack of commitment to a living wage, the practice of unpaid internships, and the need to diversify the workforce as mentioned above. Despite ethics codes and values statements, museums still suffer from lack of attention to their enforcement. Fortunately, good leadership practices, as discussed in chapter 4, can make a significant difference in responding to these concerns.

## Discussion Questions

1. How do emerging museum professionals plan their career paths in a volatile workforce environment?
2. Are performance management systems out of date? How do managers create opportunities for success?
3. Does your organization have a code of conduct or set of operating values? If so, how do they influence decisions and behaviors?
4. Is your museum preparing for generational shift through succession planning and training and development for staff?
5. Does your museum have clear policies and procedures for managing all workers, including unpaid volunteers and interns?

## Notes

1. AAM, *The Museum Workforce in the United States*, 2011, accessed September 30, 2016, at http://www.aam-us.org/docs/center-for-the-future-of-museums/museum-workforce.pdf?sfvrsn = 0.

2. Elizabeth Merritt, TrendsWatch 2016, American Alliance of Museums, 8–15, accessed September 24, 2016, at https://aam-us.org/docs/default-source/center-for-the-future-of-museums/2016_trendswatch_final_hyperlinked.pdf?Status = Temp&sfvrsn = 2.

3. Lynne Lancaster and David Stillman, *When Generations Collide* (New York: HarperCollins, 2002).

4. John Durel, "Museum Work Is Changing," *History News* (Summer 2002): 22–25.

5. Maurice Davies and Lucy Shaw, "Diversifying the Museum Workforce: The Diversify Scheme and Its Impact on Participants' Careers," in *Museum Management and Curatorship* 28, no. 2 (2013).

6. Maurice Davies, *The Tomorrow People: Entry to the Museum Workforce* (London: Museums Association, April 2007), accessed http://www.museums association.org on September 29, 2016.

7. Roger Schonfeld, Mariet Westermann, and Liam Sweeney, "Art Museum Staff Demographic Survey," Andrew W. Mellon Foundation, July 28, 2015, accessed September 30, 2016, at https://mellon.org/resources/news/articles/Diversity-American-Art-Museums/.

8. Anne Marie Gan et al., "The Gender Gap in Art Museum Directorships," 2014, AAMD, accessed September 4, 2016, https://aamd.org/our-members/from-the-field/gender-gap-report.

9. AAMD Press Release, November 17, 2015, accessed September 4, 2016, at https://aamd.org/for-the-media/press-release/united-negro-college-fund-and-association-of-art-museum-directors-launch.

10. "AAM Strategic Plan 2016–2020," accessed September 4, 2016, at http://www.aam-us.org/docs/default-source/default-document-library/english.pdf?sfvrsn=0.

11. IMLS, *What Are 21st Century Skills?* accessed September 4, 2016, https://www.imls.gov/issues/national-initiatives/museums-libraries-and-21st-century-skills.

12. Martha Morris et al., "Benchmarking Studies, 1995–2000," unpublished Internal Reports of the National Museum of American History, Smithsonian Institution.

13. Peter Drucker, *Managing the Nonprofit Organization* (New York: Harper-Collins, 1990), 150.

14. Jennifer Berkshire, "Fledgling Nonprofit Workers Love Their Jobs But Bear Financial Burdens," *Chronicle of Philanthropy*, July 22, 2012, accessed September 24, 2016, at https://www.philanthropy.com/article/Fledgling-Nonprofit-Workers/156347.

15. Geraldine Kendall, "Museums and Their Staff and Paying the Price of Low Wages," *Museums Association Journal*, January 6, 2016, accessed September 24, 2016, at http://www.museumsassociation.org/museums-journal/news-analysis/01062016-museums-and-their-staff-are-paying-the-price-of-low-wages?dm_i = 2VBX%2C8O0G%2C27LNK1%2CSIF3%2C1).

16. Smithsonian Institution Staff Satisfaction Surveys from 2008, 2010, and

2015, accessed on September 24, 2016, at https://www.si.edu/content/opanda/docs/Rpts.

17. Three articles were written by art critic Paul Richard, "Changes at the Corcoran," *Washington Post, Times Herald*, May 7, 1971, B1; "Organizing the Corcoran," *Washington Post, Times Herald*, August 25, 1971, C1; "Union Repercussions at Corcoran," *Washington Post, Times Herald*, August 31, 1971, B1.

18. *Newsweek*, "Crisis at the Corcoran," 80, no. 9 (1973): 92.

19. Phillip Kennicott, "Open Letter Berates Smithsonian's Small," *Washington Post*, January 17, 2002, C4. Author note: Small resigned his position in 2007.

20. Benjamin Sutton, "MoMA Workers Vote to Approve New Contract," *Hyperallergic*, June 22, 2015, accessed September 4, 2016, http://hyperallergic.com/216630/moma-workers-vote-to-approve-new-contract/.

21. AAM Center for the Future of Museums blog post, accessed on September 24, 2016, at http://futureofmuseums.blogspot.com/2015/06/unsafe-ideas-building-museum-worker.html.

22. Walker Information Global Network and Hudson Institute, *Commitment in the Workplace*, September 26, 2000, Hudson Institute, New York, accessed online September 30, 2016, at http://www.imrbint.com/old/imrb_pdf/global employee.pdf.

23. J. Joseph, *National Business Ethics Survey: How Employees View Ethics in Their Organizations*, 2002, Ethics Resource Center, Washington, DC.

24. *National Business Ethics Survey, 2013*, Ethics Resource Institute, accessed September 30, 2016, at http://www.ethics.org/research/nbes/nbes-reports/nbes-2013.

## CHAPTER FOUR
# LEADERSHIP IN MUSEUMS

Project management systems in museums are dependent on strong leadership commitment. This chapter will examine the best practices in leadership today and how these impact the success of projects. The following topics will be covered:

- leadership defined

- twenty-first-century leadership skills

- ethics and decision making

- models of museum leadership

## Leadership Defined

Understanding the impact and meaning of leadership in the modern organization is the subject of constant debate. Today we look at leadership from many angles, including political, social, economic, and cultural. Leaders have tremendous impact on the success or failure of all sectors of our society. They are at their best when they influence the work of others toward positive end goals. This chapter will look at the theory and practice of leadership in nonprofits and museums, but will reference ideas and experiences from for-profit studies as well. A good way to begin is to determine how leaders and managers differ. The difference between leadership and management has been debated for many years, and the distinction needs to be explored. Although leadership is what we all are looking for to guide our organizations through turbulent times, competent managers are needed as well.[1]

The traditional thinking is that managers "do things right," such as:

- organize work

- develop plans

- hire and train staff

- evaluate programs and staff

- acquire resources

- communicate

- analyze needs/results

- make decisions

But what do leaders do that is different? They "do the right things," such as:

- create vision and positive scenarios for the future

- have passion

- take risks and encourage others to do so

- consider the impact of their actions: see the big picture

- develop basic values

- empower and stretch staff

- listen, facilitate, and coach

- seek shared values and common vision

Clearly there is a distinction between leaders and managers. We know, however, that these traits can be blended in individuals. Depending on the situation that faces the organization, a visionary leader may also need to plan, supervise, and evaluate individuals in the workplace. Managers can also step out of their administrative role to take risks and dream big about the changes needed in the organization. Project management systems require both leadership and management to succeed. We will look at factors that compel museums to seek these types of individuals. As we face an unstable and challenging world, we need leaders at all levels of the organization.

## Situational Leadership

Closely related to the above definition is a leadership and management theory originally developed by Professor Paul Hersey in the late 1960s. In defining the evolution of the relationship between the employee and the supervisor, there is a continuum of oversight based on the relationship between behaviors and tasks. As illustrated in figure 4.1, the progression of direction and oversight changes with the learning and capabilities of the employee. In quadrant 1 (sergeant), the supervisor is closely directing the work of the new worker. They must move from being tough to being supportive over time. In quadrant 2 (coach), the supervisor is frequently checking for understanding of the work, providing motivation and guidance. Moving to quadrant 3, the supervisor (facilitator) provides the tools and other resources to do the work, while in the fourth

**Figure 4.1. Situational leadership. Adapted from Hersey, Blanchard and Johnson,** *Management of Organizational Behavior.*

quadrant, the supervisor is a delegator, establishing the end goal while the employee works at their own pace with little or no oversight. Clearly, then, not all employees should be treated with the same level of supervision. Their level of readiness, confidence, and skill level will change. Although this is straightforward, it can be stressful for the manager who may be expected to treat everyone equally. This only adds to the complexity of workplace dynamics.[2]

## Modern Leadership Theory

Much has been written in business literature about leadership. Looking at theories that have been developed since the early 1990s, we see a shift in emphasis from a top-down directive approach to the behavioral management systems as described in chapter 1. A few examples will be outlined here as they continue to resonate with current leadership challenges. Jim Collins in his seminal work *Built to Last* (coauthored with Jerry Porras) described successful company leaders as the creators of Big Hairy Audacious Goals (BHAG). At the same time, these companies demonstrated outstanding success over a one-hundred-year period due to a strong internal culture, an ability to push for innovation while preserving core strengths, a reliance on enduring values, and a focus on homegrown management.[3] Collins also continued to study corporate and nonprofit organizations through the 1990s. He observed a new type of leader who is selfless, humble, determined, and gives credit to others. The "Level 5" leader takes responsibility, has a strong and determined will to see the organization succeed, but consistently gives credit to others.[4]

Daniel Goleman of Harvard University defined enduring characteristics of effective leadership in his writings on emotional intelligence. In the corporate setting, he found that success was equated with personalities who demonstrated self-awareness, self-regulation, motivation, empathy, and social skills. All of these traits are defined by trustworthiness, openness to change, optimism, commitment, cross-cultural sensitivity, and teambuilding.[5] Rather than intellectual prowess, the successful leader needs to exhibit personal traits that are focused on group behavior and individual awareness. Goleman continued to write about the importance of focus in leadership. He speaks of self-awareness, empathy in understanding other perspectives, and responsiveness to the needs of others.

The higher up you get in the organization the more likely you won't be focused and empathetic. Therefore, understanding the wider world, being a good listener, and being tuned in to group dynamics will lead to more innovation on the part of staff.

Peter Senge of MIT defined important success criteria in his writings about learning organizations. The emphasis on a holistic approach includes:

- systems thinking: understanding the big picture

- personal mastery: self-knowledge

- mental models: recognizing and overcoming biases in thinking

- shared vision: creating a vision that all employees can buy into

- team learning: a culture of analyzing lessons learned

The above characteristics emphasize a new way of working, which both enlists all staff in managing the organization and promotes the ability to learn from experiences. Similar to Goleman, he observed that leaders need to have a strong sense of self both personally and professionally. The reference to mental models is of value in overcoming misunderstandings based on ingrained assumptions about the attitudes of colleagues in the workplace. Senge's most lasting theory is the emphasis on team learning, where reflection on program goals and work process can lead to improvements. For example, in the museum field a process of team evaluation of successes and failures in exhibition projects leads to improvements for the future.[6]

## Twenty-First-Century Leadership Skills

The theories espoused by Collins, Goleman, and Senge continue to be of relevance in the twenty-first-century workplace, including museums. In fact, one of the biggest challenges for museums is being able to master change, and their theories are most supportive of this approach. Another management guru who has espoused a practical approach to leading change is John Kotter of Harvard. Kotter's work in the 1990s continues to influence organizations today. His ideas include creating a sense of urgency, building a guiding coalition of internal change agents, creating the capacity to implement change among staff members, and reinforcing the new approaches in the culture of the organization.[7] As in the for-profit sector, change is a constant issue for all museums. As our environment evolves and presents new challenges, the museum needs to adapt. Economic downturns can result in layoffs, hiring freezes, as well as mergers and reorganizations. Environmental disasters can cause major impacts that could hamper operations. Political changes, competition from other museums and cultural attractions, or neighborhood development can put new pressures on leadership. Likewise, a successful fund-raising campaign can bring unexpected resources to create new programs, while shifts in communications technology such as social media and smartphones demand new skills and ways of working with audiences. Other changes include leadership transitions or loss of a key staff member. The world of modern change literature has defined this state of constant change as VUCA, one that is volatile, uncertain, complex, and ambiguous. Organizations that are proactive in dealing with this challenge need to take the following steps:[8]

- Make decisions based on sound data.

- Seek a diversity of ideas and views.

- Experiment with solutions.

- Create a resource reserve for unexpected downturns.

This approach is similar to the theory of adaptive leadership as described by Heifetz and Laurie in 2009.[9] Dealing with change requires a fast-paced approach, one based on an organization-wide collaboration. Instead of taking months to develop a new strategic plan, for example, the organization should focus on experimental thinking and a redesign of the cumbersome processes. Moving quickly is stressful. Leaders should infuse the process with empathy, holding direct and courageous conversations that challenge the status quo without laying blame. Group discussions should focus on solutions and sets of options to explore. Managing inevitable conflicts requires a focus on facts, not opinions. From this should evolve a set of decision criteria. The application of this approach should allow for more strategic thinking, as we discussed in chapter 2. The following are the key responsblities of the adaptive leaders and reflect those of strategic thinking.

- protection

- direction

- orientation

- managing conflict

- shaping norms

The above leadership skills are all necessary. The successful museum needs to develop strategic thinkers that willingly step up and take on change. Moving outside one's defined role on the organization chart to provide leadership on projects or even to assist with short-term problem solving is a twenty-first-century skill. Leaders at all levels need to focus on relationship building among internal and external stakeholders, and empathy should underlie these relationships. We need to adopt effective communications in all forms (oral, written, and digital). In fact, in our digital world the individual who is fluent in creating and understanding performance metrics will be increasingly valued. The adaptive practices of Heifetz are also important when we use rapid prototyping to test new ideas for interpretive programs and new audiences. And all staff need to be able to see the big-picture goals of the organization and create change based on team analysis of projects, as described in Senge's "learning organization."[10]

## Ethics and Decision Making

In chapter 3 we reviewed best practices in building a productive staff and focused on the concerns and real-world issues of staff satisfaction, values, and ethics. These challenges are compounded by the realities of our complex world. Not only do we need to be adaptive leaders in a learning organization, we also must deeply understand the psychological relationship between leaders and their employees. *Harvard Business Review* published an article regarding trust in leadership, which cited a survey of thirty companies. The results revealed that at least 50 percent of staff doesn't trust their leaders.[11] The consequence of this leads to lack of productivity, stress, and turnover. Willingness to trust is closely related to one's ability to take risks, their sense of self-satisfaction, and the power they may hold in the organization. Also, if the issues are high stakes, trust is harder. An organization that openly stresses values of candor, integrity, and fairness and concern for employees is best.

Dealing with the results of economic recessions and lack of jobs makes it harder for organizations to build loyalty, and ethics becomes more important in building trust. The Ethics Resource Institute has conducted research on the role of the leader in the workplace.[12]

Their findings reveal that employees had high regard for top leaders and supervisors at all levels when they demonstrated respect for all staff, upheld standards, kept promises, shared credit for success, handled crises well, and assured ethical policies were in place. In addition, these leaders followed up on violations of ethics and values codes and took needed action. When we consider some of the problems of museums in recent years, it is clear there is justification for ethical behavior. Financial mismanagement, excessively high salaries of directors, collections deaccession and sale to cover operations, undue donor influence, ambitious building expansions, and investment policies that support publically harmful businesses such as oil companies can all lead to mistrust in the workplace.

### Decision Making

Decision making and ethics are related. The bottom line is a need to be consistent, open, and fair. Policies set guidelines for decisions such as collections management, fund-raising, finance, or personnel and the code of ethics. These guide the board and staff in making sound decisions. Those that affect the mission, resources, or reputation of the museum must be carefully taken. They can have profound impact, and need to be well documented and carefully crafted. A fair process is one that includes as many stakeholders as possible, one that is shared widely, and one in which staff members understand their role in executing decisions. However, organizations often tend to keep high-stakes decisions close to the vest or simply fail to share the information in a timely and clear manner. For example, the unilateral decision to censor the *Hide/Seek* exhibition at the National Portrait Gallery in 2010 created a firestorm of concern and undermined the credibility of the Smithsonian leadership. Given the findings about ethics and trust, this case was particularly instructive. Policies were in place for review of controversial exhibition content, including who was to make the ultimate decisions, but evidently they were not followed.[13]

The decision process does not always require consensus. A continuum of participation is customary depending on the stakes involved (see figure 4.2). If the decision has wide impact, is costly and long term, then a consensus process can be employed. If a decision is in regard to an imminent crisis or threat, then the authoritative method makes the most sense. In the middle are many of the types of decisions that need to be made in the museum, and these are for the most part the prerogative of the leader, after gathering data and consulting with affected stakeholders. In the case of the Smithsonian's *Hide/Seek* exhibition, it is probable that the consultative approach would have been desirable. In many cases, though, the emotional side of decisions cannot be controlled by any process but could be significantly mitigated. Other approaches to decision making involve a weighted matrix, which allows the museum to assess factors that are most important, based on cost, mission, and risk, similar to the Matrix Map approach discussed in chapter 2. In this approach the program in question can be placed on a continuum of risk and reward given its importance based on defined criteria.

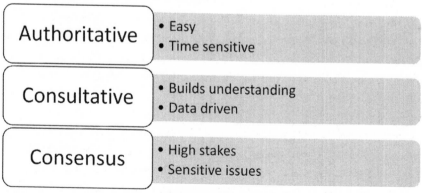

**Figure 4.2. Continuum of participation. Courtesy of the author.**

### Leadership Accountability and Performance Management

Considering new modes of decision making and ethical guidelines that are fair minded and inclusive, how are we able to assure our leaders and supervisors are accountable for their actions? The process of annual performance reviews is one way. Although leaders are accustomed to evaluating the output of staff, there is value in having a leadership assessment program. Known as a 360-degree evaluation, these programs involve gathering feedback from peers, direct reports, and senior management. They are almost always confidential in nature and allow for honest feedback to be shared with the individual leader. Alongside the ethics, values, and code of conduct adopted by the museum, this approach can assure an accountable system.

An alternative approach to measuring success for leadership is to assess the way that values statements impact the behavior of the organization. For example, leadership that says "yes" to new ideas and seeks open dialog among board and staff without fear is a measure for the San Diego Museum of Man's "adventurous" value.[14]

## Models of Museum Leadership

What are the key issues for museum leadership today? There are many critical issues facing museum leaders that need action, including improved board/staff relations, marketing and fund-raising, diversity and community engagement, succession planning, organizational change, collections, facilities, and financial sustainability. The best museum leaders are attentive to the balance of internal and external demands, comfortable with ambiguity, provide staff learning opportunities, surround themselves with strength, and keep their ego in check. As early as the 1990s there were directors actively seeking feedback in operations and planning as a bottom-up approach, delegating decisions to front-line staff and building cross-functional teams.[15]

What are the primary functions of museum directors? It is estimated that the director spends about 50 percent of their time working with the board. This includes planning, developing policies, working with outside organizations, developing and monitoring budgets, and fund-raising. The board relationship is extremely important. Because the board is legally liable for managing and protecting the assets in support of the mission, they need to take their role seriously. We hear stories of how this doesn't work. Boards are not engaged, do not understand their role, and do not have the decision systems in place to be effective.[16] Thus, building the board relationship is likely the most important function for a director. Challenge them with problems to solve, get to know their interests and skills, and engage them in seeking resources to support the museum. It is important to provide excellent communications, orientation and updates, and clear expectations in the form of position descriptions. Importantly, they need to be given thanks and credit for the good things that happen at the museum. The level of board involvement is also a matter of bylaws and of the nature of the board members themselves. Clearly they should not be in a position to micromanage the daily operations. Building trust in the director is the first step. Setting parameters for when the board needs to be involved in decisions is fundamental. Beyond the board relationship are many other leadership duties, as outlined below.

- create vision

- guide strategic and annual operational planning

- fund-raising

- work with communities

- build and protect collections and facilities

- develop policies and procedures

- create quality programs

- communications: internal and external

- evaluate progress: based on performance measure

Looking at these duties, we can see the extraordinary demands that are placed on museum leaders today. Depending on the needs of the museum, the leader divided his or her time in support of all of these functions and hopefully delegates many of them to the museum staff.

Beyond these duties, a modern museum leader also needs to operate with other twenty-first-century skills such as the following:

- mobilize change efforts

- focus on the values of the museum

- invest in staff development/allow for risk taking

- seek collaboration with external partners

- listen and be empathetic

- seek out and encourage grassroots leaders

- recognize and reward individual and team contributions

As University of Virginia professor Jeanne Liedtka has outlined in her writing on design thinking, the new leader in either the for-profit or nonprofit world excels when they have a learning mindset, take risks, experiment, have a deep connection to the customer or audience, and are willing to "tell the hard truth about current reality and be optimistic about the future."[17]

How can museum leaders adapt these traits along with so many other traditional responsibilities? The most successful leaders are able to surround themselves with talented staff, create a sense of work-life balance, and develop incredible discipline in execution.

### Model Museum Leaders

Who are some of the individuals that have embraced the qualities that are described above? Robert Janes led the organizational transformation of the Glenbow Museum in Calgary, Alberta, Canada, in the 1990s. Reacting to a loss of government funding, the Glenbow faced layoffs and other reductions in programs. Janes was convinced that a new form of organization—one that was inclusive and collaborative—was needed to transform the museum. A new strategic plan for the museum included creating a community service focus, a business model that included a mix of revenue sources, active deaccessioning of non–mission-related collections, business process simplification, and new commercial enterprises. A new museum school opened opportunities for teachers to move the classroom to the museum.[18] Janes and his staff defined a set of operational principles that balanced freedom and responsibility. These included making decisions based on the museum's goals and strategies; every individual understanding their role and expected results; free and open communication; and encouragement to act with thoughtful risk taking. Senior leaders were expected to model mutual trust, confidence, and respect among all staff. The museum's "blueprint for change" played out over a decade. One of the most challenging pillars of this change was the new organizational structure. Reorganization can be stressful for staff. Eighteen functional departments were collapsed into six multidisciplinary units. This design was successful for several years before tweaking the structure was needed. This involved the combination of two functional units under one senior manager. Another interesting outcome was that the library and archives division determined to rotate leadership of the unit as a self-managed team; certainly this was not something that would have happened without the model of collaboration set by Janes.[19]

The leadership of Chase Rynd, executive director at the National Building Museum in Washington, DC, also reflects these new traits. Trained as an art historian, Rynd took over at the museum in 2003. He freely admits that the job involved a learning curve to absorb the topic of building as well as nurturing the staff. The museum has been a leader in exhibitions and programs that tackle environmental sustainability and community development. Rynd has exercised good listening skills, consistently sought staff feedback, and encouraged experimental programs while providing learning opportunities for staff. He is not averse to putting in time at the information desk or in leading tours. He has also worked to create broad input from stakeholders in decision making and supporting his staff in developing exhibition programs.[20]

Jane Werner, director of the Children's Museum of Pittsburgh, was trained as an educator and artist. An example of the modern leader who is both realist and optimist, Werner and her team created one of the best examples of a community-based museum in the country. Located in an economically challenged area of the city, the museum consistently reached out to neighbors and other organizations in the city to create learning opportunities for young audiences. The "maker space" movement is a central feature of their programming. In addition, the museum houses non-profit groups with compatible missions. Staff of the museum are nurtured and encouraged to take risks in developing programs that provide community leadership development projects, such as those involving local teens. Werner's work has been recognized on a national basis. In 2016 the museum was awarded a grant by the Google Foundation for replicating their "maker spaces" in organizations and schools across the country.[21]

G. Rollie Adams was appointed CEO of the Strong Museum in Rochester, New York, in 1986, where he was an early adopter of leadership and management best practices. He instituted Total Quality Management approaches with a focus on team-based management and customer service training for staff. He also created a "boundryless" approach to organizing work.[22] Constantly revolving teams of staff were assigned to work on a variety of projects. Similar to the organization of the Glenbow Museum in Alberta, Canada, the Strong teams were focused on operations, process improvement, and special projects. The museum revised its mission to serve families and children and eventually to become the National Museum of Play, dedicated to collecting, researching, and interpreting the topic. The museum has been successful in building its financial base, expanding facilities, and serving the community in innovative ways.[23]

In reflecting on the work of these leaders, there are some common threads. Each has devoted a considerable number of years to their positions. They have consistently reinvented their museums with new ideas that resonate with communities. They can be described as risk takers and champions of change. And importantly they are respectful and supportive of their staff.

## Preparing New Museum Leaders

The demographics of the early twenty-first century point to the rapidly retiring baby boom generation. These retirements are leaving vacancies at a rapid rate. Over one-third of art museum directors are expected to retire by 2020. Seeking replacements has been difficult, and some museums are looking at crossover candidates. Such individuals are often from arts, higher education, business, or other nonprofit organizations. Despite this lack of museum experience, many of these individuals bring new perspectives to challenged organizations.[24] If we are seeking to prepare existing staff in our museums for leadership roles, we need to explore opportunities for staff development.

How do managers become leaders? No organization can afford to ignore the importance of empowering staff to take on leadership roles. This is important for succession planning and for implementing the adaptive processes mentioned above. The need for leadership at all levels of the organization can be met through acknowledging the skills needed. This is particularly important in the project management arena. Most often project managers are assigned to this task because of their specialized experience in a particular function such as curatorial, education, or collections management. These individuals need to move from being specialists to generalists, from consideration of tactics to strategies, and to learn diplomacy and problem solving. These skills can be groomed with both specialized training and on-the-job opportunities. Exposure to the broad workings of the organization through assignment to cross-functional task forces, or to a support position to a senior leader, can add significantly to the individual's readiness. In fact, museums should consider what some in the corporate world are now looking for: nontraditional skills such as strategic thinking, emergent leadership, stepping up to part-time projects, a sense of responsibility, and humility.[25]

*Training*

There are many leadership and ethics training programs in colleges and universities, not just for business leaders but also nonprofits. Similar training is offered at the Center for Creative Leadership in Greensboro, North Carolina, and the Aspen Institute in Colorado. Museum studies programs are increasingly adding leadership and management courses to their programs. Other museum leadership training includes the Museum Leadership Institute underwritten by the Getty at Claremont University in California, Bank Street College in New York, and Columbia University's Center for Curatorial Leadership, to name a few. Individual museums such as the Smithsonian and the Victoria & Albert Museum in Great Britain have developed leadership development programs for those staff that may one day succeed existing leaders. Leadership training is now a regular part of the programming of the American Alliance of Museums, American Association for State and Local History, and other regional associations. The Museum Trustee Association also has programs that improve understanding of governing board responsibilities and managing the process of recruitment, orientation, and improved communications with staff, especially the director. Despite these programs there are still thousands of museum workers who could benefit from training, and they are on their own with this. Fortunately, there are growing numbers of online and face-to-face continuing education training courses for museum professionals. In our networked world, it is easier to access individuals to share information about best practices. Despite these many options for moving up the ladder, the best training today is actual on-the-job experience. A study conducted by social networking site LinkedIn revealed that the best predictor of landing a top leadership position was obtaining experience in several functional areas of a business.[26] This speaks to the need for cross-training and the worker's willingness to move within the organization even if it does not mean a promotion. Fortunately, project management offers an opportunity for this.

## Discussion Questions

1. How does your museum address the issue of leadership development? Think of ways that this could be improved in the future.
2. How does your museum manage change? Think of a recent situation that demanded top leadership assistance in moving through a change effort. What was learned from this experience?
3. What type of decision-making systems do you need for specific situations, such as a new building for your museum? Consider the continuum of participation. How would you use these variations for the types of decisions facing your workplace today?

## Notes

1. This distinction was detailed in the work of Warren Bennis, *On Becoming a Leader* (New York: Addison Wesley, 1989).
2. Ken Blanchard and Paul Hersey, *Management of Organizational Behavior* (New York: Prentice Hall, 1972).

3. Jim Collins and Jerry Porras, *Built to Last* (New York: HarperBusiness, 1994).

4. Jim Collins, "Level 5 Leadership: The Triumph of Humility and Fierce Resolve," *Harvard Business Review* (January 2001): 19–28.

5. Daniel Goleman, "What Makes a Leader?" *Harvard Business Review* 78, no. 6 (November–December 1998): 93–102.

6. Peter Senge, *The Fifth Discipline* (New York: Doubleday, 1990).

7. John Kotter, *Leading Change* (Boston: Harvard Business School Press, 1996).

8. Nathan Bennett and James Lemoine, "What VUCA Really Means for You," *Harvard Business Review* (January–February 2014), hbr.org accessed August 21, 2016.

9. Ronald Heifetz and Donald Laurie, *The Practice of Adaptive Leadership* (Boston: Harvard Business Press, 2009).

10. Marsha Semmel, "Museum Leadership in a Hyper-Connected World," *Museum* (May-June 2015): 65–66.

11. Robert F. Hurley, "The Decision to Trust," *Harvard Business Review* (September 2006): 55–61.

12. "Ethical Leadership," Ethics Research Institute, accessed September 11, 2016, http://www.ethics.org/eci/research/eci-research/nbes/nbes-reports/ethical-leadership.

13. Sheryl Stolberg and Kate Taylor, "Wounded in Crossfire of a Capital Culture War," *New York Times*, March 30, 2011, accessed September 18, 2016, at http://www.nytimes.com/2011/04/03/arts/design/g-wayne-clough-and-the-smithsonian-new-culture-war.html.

14. "A Blueprint for Success: Strategic Plan 2012–2015," San Diego Museum of Man, 31, accessed on September 26, 2016, at http://www.museumofman.org/sites/default/files/sdmom_stratplan.pdf.

15. Martha Morris, "1995 Survey on Strategic Planning, Organizational Change, and Quality Management," an informal, unpublished study of twenty-nine US museums conducted by the National Museum of American History Smithsonian Institution, 1995.

16. Maureen Robinson, *Nonprofit Boards That Work* (New York: Wiley, 2000).

17. Jeanne Liedtka, "A New Leadership Mindset," presentation at HRPS, accessed September 18, 2016, http://c.ymcdn.com/sites/www.hrps.org/resource/resmgr/ff11_presentations/jeanne_liedtka_.pdf

18. Robert Janes, *Museums and the Paradox of Change* (Calgary: Glenbow Museum and the University of Calgary Press, 1997), 30.

19. Janes, *Museums and the Paradox of Change*, 250–53.

20. Personal interview of Chase Rynd by author, February 26, 2010.

21. Anne Bergeron and Beth Tuttle, *Magnetic: The Art and Science of Engagement* (Washington, DC: AAM Press, 2013), 125–34.

22. General Electric CEO Jack Welch developed the term *boundryless* in 1990. Subsequently, Wharton professors Larry Hirschhorn and Thomas Gilmore wrote an article in *Harvard Business Review*, "The New Boundaries of the Boundryless Company" (May–June 1992): 104–15.

23. Adams shared much of his "reinvention" practices in a keynote presentation at the Midatlantic Association of Museums Building Museums™ conference in Washington, DC, in 2007. Adams also had several informal conversations with the author regarding the museum's growth beginning in the 1990s through 2007.

24. Julia Halperin, "As a Generation of Directors Reaches Retirement, Fresh Faces Prepare to Take over US Museums," *Art Newspaper*, June 2, 2015, accessed September 12, 2016, at http://theartnewspaper.com/news/museums/fresh-faces -set-to-take-over-at-the-top-/.

25. Thomas L. Friedman, "How to Get a Job at Google," *New York Times*, February 22, 2014, accessed September 12, 2016, http://www.nytimes.com/ 2014/02/23/opinion/sunday/friedman-how-to-get-a-job-at-google.html?_r = 0 http://www.nytimes.com/2014/02/23/opinion/sunday/friedman-how-to-get-a -job-at-google.html?_r = 0.

26. Neil Irwin, "How to Become a CEO? The Quickest Path Is a Winding One," *New York Times*, accessed September 11, 2016, http://www.nytimes.com/ 2016/09/11/upshot/how-to-become-a-ceo-the-quickest-path-is-a-winding -one.html?_r = 0.

# PROJECT MANAGEMENT IN MUSEUMS

This chapter will cover the nature of project management systems and the early planning phases that are considered best practices in the field. The following chapters cover the development of projects and the role of teams in their success. Project management has been an important tool in organizations since the 1950s when manufacturing, construction, government, and service industries adopted this approach for its emphasis on efficiency and quality. Many large corporations such as IBM, Google, Microsoft, and Disney do most of their work on a project basis. This approach is successfully used in the building industries and in manufacturing, as there is a heavy design and production component that requires the acquisition of skilled resources and monitoring progress over time. Project management is a methodical and systematic approach but relies very heavily on people working in a collaborative planning and implementation process. Think back to chapter 1 where we examined the scientific and behavioral theories of management. Both of these are critical to the implementation of project management. In nonprofits and museums in particular where staff and other stakeholders have a significant voice, the use of these techniques has the potential to engage employees in a rewarding manner. And in an era of downsizing and increasing competition, museums need to adopt streamlined operations. Much like the for-profit sector, museums use project management to organize work around outcomes that are customer focused and mission based. The application of the approach is now so widespread in business and nonprofits that it has spawned continuing education and formal university degree programs. The Project Management Institute now offers certification in the field for thousands of individuals in all sectors of our economy, including museum personnel.[1] The following represent the types of core museum programs that are good candidates for project management approaches:

- renovation, expansion, and new building

- exhibitions and public programs

- collections moves

- collections inventory and digitization

- special events

- conservation treatment

- information systems development

Project management is defined as a work activity leading to a distinct product within a defined time frame with dedicated resources. It often involves collaboration of several functional units of the organization and outside service providers working together. One of the most important factors is that it is a *disciplined system*. This creates an immediate challenge for some museums that are less inclined to adopt business practices. Museum staff is often more interested in professional standards, collections research, innovative design, and other "creative" activities. Thus they have been slow to use this approach. The Smithsonian Institution has been a leader in this effort over the past twenty-five years, and several of their member museums now have dedicated project management staff. Building such a formal program provides a community of practice and common terminology and process within the museums and across the institution.

In research conducted by the National Museum of American History in the late 1990s, over thirty museums surveyed indicated they were using a form of project management, particularly for exhibition development.[2] These museums used cross-functional teams, had a central office to monitor project progress, and developed a formal process to launch the projects including spelling out roles and responsibilities. Many of these museums had dedicated project managers on staff. In many cases museums with full-time project managers had large staff numbers (over fifty), yet in all instances despite their size a staff member was assigned to coordinate the planning and implementation of special projects.

## The Project Life Cycle

Projects have a life cycle that can be defined as conception/selection, planning, implementation, and evaluation (see figure 5.1). The conceptual phase links the project to the organization's strategic plan and goals. For example, idea generation for exhibitions is a phase that involves brainstorming and visitor feedback in order to assure that a project is going to resonate with audiences and line up with the museum's vision and mission. The planning phase involves the detailing of scope, schedule, budget, and team development. Operational policies and systems of reporting on progress guide the implementation phase. It is here where the heart of the work occurs and constant vigilance is needed to accommodate unexpected events that will alter the success of the plan. Evaluation is done at the end of the project, yet the rubrics that guide this activity are established at the outset. Here the team will engage in detailed quantitative and qualitative analysis of success or failure of the project.

**Figure 5.1.  Project life cycle. Courtesy of the author.**

## Feasibility Phase

Before launching a project, the museum needs to analyze the need and its viability. No project should go forward without a serious assessment of its feasibility. As a part of strategic planning, this phase exists to assure that any initiative undertaken is not doomed to fail. Chapter 2 outlined some options for assessing the profitability and mission delivery of strategic goals and objectives using a Matrix Map. That approach is useful in assessing the value of existing program areas as well as in judging new project ideas. Generally speaking, individual projects are launched after a detailed review and approval process takes place. Guidelines for the process are also developed using past successes as the model. Some museum guidelines are merely checklists of activities, while others go into greater detail, including definition of roles and responsibilities of key players.

In conducting a feasibility study for museum projects, it is important to involve knowledgeable staff. In the case of an exhibition project, the key players should include content specialists (curators), audience advocates/educators, collections managers, exhibition designers, facilities, technology, and finance and fund-raising staff. A project manager or other staff member with experience in exhibitions should coordinate the review. Projects with much larger scope than a single exhibition, such as a new building project, will include external advisors that can assess the market for a new venture and develop an assessment of donor interest in a capital campaign. In these cases economic impact studies and comprehensive business plans will be common. In either case the viability of the project must look at stakeholder needs and assumptions about audiences, internal capacity, staffing and financial strengths and weaknesses, security and accessibility, the competing needs of other approved projects, and post-project sustainability.

Calculating the risk of a project is critical. In the case of a major project, the museum is wise to consider what might go wrong. Known as the "what if" approach, this phase can reveal a number of potential problems. What if your major donor pulls out? What if the cost of producing an exhibition suddenly escalates? What if another museum opens in your community, drawing away your visitors? What if a natural disaster occurs in your region? Depending on the size of the project, developing scenarios to mitigate risk will help in making sound decisions about going forward.

Initiatives that may require this type of analysis include projects that involve new external partners, new technology, or new areas of scholarship, for example. Launching a new website, partnering with other museums, or developing a new area of research and collecting where there is not a lot of in-house experience requires a more careful risk analysis. Models of assessing risk are available in a Technical Leaflet published by the AASLH in 2012. This publication lays out ideas for testing what might happen given the size of the project, its importance, the stability of resources, and application of untested technology systems, for example.[3]

Although it is assumed that all projects are born from the goals and objectives of the museum's approved strategic plan, there will be new ideas that can and should be considered. Considerations should include the need to link the proposal to the museum's mission and its ability to leverage ongoing strategic goals. Suppressing the desire to say "It's a great idea, let's do it" without some consideration of impact on other work is a big mistake. Questions that should be asked include: Why do this project, and if so, when is the best time? What are the expected results? How will we measure success? Who are the primary stakeholders involved in this project, and how do we assess their needs? What assumptions do we need to consider, such as reliance on specific collections, staff members, an available space on the exhibition schedule, or the time available to complete the project? Can we be sure we are not approving something just because it is a popular idea of the director, board chair, or other key decision maker?

Assuring resources are available requires developing a preliminary budget. These numbers should only serve as a placeholder since further detailing of the project will reveal a more exact set of numbers. However, there is a delicate balance here. The museum should feel confident enough with the budget to make a reasonable no-go/go decision. And once approved making any dramatic changes in the scope of the project will have a certain impact on budget. The early phases of planning are the time to make adjustments. Once in the implementation phase these adjustments are more difficult. Often a cost/benefit analysis will help (see figure 5.2). If we do this project, will it result in significant advancement of our strategic plan? Or will we find that we have invested time in a project that has little impact? One area that also needs to be considered but is often overlooked in the excitement of a new idea is the "opportunity

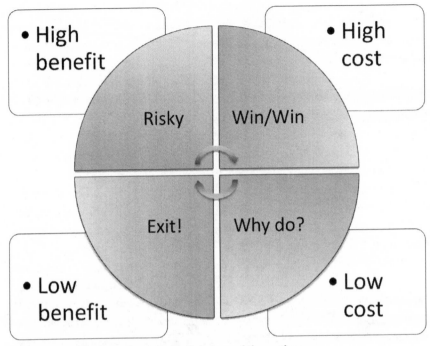

**Figure 5.2. Cost/benefit analysis. Courtesy of the author.**

cost." Simply stated, what are we giving up by taking on a new project? Are we setting aside work on collections care or accession backlogs to divert resources to a new public program or exhibition? In fact, this is probably one of the most important criteria for museums today. We are short staffed with constrained budgets. Deciding to accept a blockbuster traveling exhibition might mean that we are risking compromising standards of care. Not a good trade-off, for sure. One factor that museums today almost always need to consider is the funding source. A project is not likely to be approved without some assurance that money is there to pay for it. Thus, development staff needs to play a role in this feasibility phase.

Often guiding the decision process is an all-important thematic framework. All museums should work with a set of intellectual themes to guide their interpretive plans. These are typically developed in the strategic planning process. Themes can be organized by audiences, by community interests, by social movements, or by collection strengths. This will vary from museum to museum. A community-based museum would develop projects in collaboration with local audiences. Stakeholder interests can drive the selection process. Community members may even serve to curate exhibitions. In most museums, core staff develops exhibitions and programs. Although curators may take the lead with interpretive programs, the museum should form a planning team or working group to develop themes and overarching educational messages. This team, augmented by outside experts including historians and designers or media specialists, will bring new ideas to the table. Diverse viewpoints are critical. As ideas are debated and explored, assure that plenty of time is set aside for this work. In considering the audience, these plans should include ways to incorporate critical thinking, elaborate on public debate, and provide opportunities to personalize the visitor's experience in the museum.[4]

Visitor experience components include exhibitions, public programs, interactives, special events, and outreach activities. Creating an overarching plan linked to the fulfillment of mission and vision is ideal. Specific project ideas can be generated around themes or other priority frameworks or can be responsive to input from the community stakeholders. An example might be the recognition of a key local event or anniversary. Visitor research and demographic data created during strategic planning can also reveal important ideas for new interpretive projects. Other types of projects relate to core goals, such as new areas of collecting, collections preservation and access, and digital outreach. In the majority of cases, any project being pursued should be in the context of the strategic plan, its vision and goals (see figure 5.3).

## Approving the Project

Review and selection of projects will usually involve either internal staff or possibly board members and external advisors. A tiered system involves

**Figure 5.3. Context of projects. Courtesy of the author.**

several rounds of review before final approval. Decision-making committees are composed of affected stakeholders on the staff at a minimum.
The final decision may be the responsibility of the director or the board,
but levels of internal review can avoid problems. Consistency in the process is critical. Additionally, a transparent process will do much to assure
buy-in by staff. Policies should be developed that outline the decision
criteria, the process of review, and the final decision makers. If exceptions
occur or controversy is associated with the project idea, a process to
resolve or accommodate these circumstances is important. An example
might be a museum exhibition or program that will potentially incur public protests or audience criticism. The museum should be ready to deal
with this issue well in advance of implementation.

My research on the exhibition development process revealed that
museums are regularly forming decision-making committees that are
cross-functional, that function as both an approving body as well as providing ongoing oversight for projects as they develop. For example, in the
late 1990s the Missouri Historical Society used a Research and Program
Committee to review proposals developed by teams. Criteria for review
included scholarship, mission, exhibition strategy, complementary programming, audience appeal, and resource needs.[5] A similar approach is
customarily used in other museums. The National Museum of American
History has a staff exhibits development committee comprised of curators,
educators, and programmers and project managers serving to review ideas
and mentor staff through the proposal development phase.[6]

Similarly, in implementing a new project management approach at
the Nebraska State Historical Society, all projects (not just exhibitions)
require completion of a Project Proposal Form (see Appendix F). The
society is actively engaged in implementing project management systems
under the direction of CEO Trevor Jones. As a certified project management expert (PMP from the Project Management Institute), Jones is a
true believer in the importance of these techniques. The proposal form is
based on one he developed while serving as a division director at the
Kentucky Historical Society. It is used to vet and informally charter projects. He feels that the form serves to "build Project Management principles into the process without being too intimidating." The form is a
simple way to give staff an opportunity to share their good ideas and at

the same time to think "critically about measurable results and deliverables." Staff members submit the form for discussion with their supervisor, and then once approved it goes to the CEO and the senior division directors for vetting. If the idea is approved then a project manager will be assigned. Jones sees this as the single most important document for decision making as it forces the organization to think about outcomes and resources.[7]

Not all museums have a highly structured approach to decision making. An example of how some museums approach the decision process was detailed in a *New York Times* article in August 2016 that featured several small to midsized art museums in the Northeast region. For example, the Bruce Museum in Greenwich, Connecticut, plans several years in advance by holding "program forums" to brainstorm ideas for exhibitions. Decisions are based on the availability of artwork, audience appeal, and museum mission.[8] In a volatile world underscored by changes in the economy, society, and technological advances, museums are increasingly amenable to alter or drop a bureaucratic decision process. More flexibility is needed in an ever-changing world. The need to do short-term projects that are responsive to public policy, social change, or audience demands requires a template for planning that will accommodate these opportunities. Sometimes the response can be a small exhibition case or a web-based program, or more often a public program. Examples of these types of projects will be covered in later chapters.

## Discussion Questions

1. How does your museum develop project ideas? Is there a policy in place? Do you have a clear outline of who is responsible for these decisions?

2. How do you go about developing a program plan that incorporates visionary themes and responds to visitor experience expectations?

3. How does feasibility and risk analysis work with small museums? Do they need to invest in the up-front time and cost associated with moving forward with a project?

## Notes

1. The Project Management Institute accessed at www.pmi.org, October 30, 2016.

2. Martha Morris, "Recent Trends in Exhibition Development," in *Exhibitionist*, National Association of Museum Exhibitions 21, no. 1 (2002): 8–12.

3. Steven Hoskins, "Calculating Risk: A Guide to Project Management for History Professionals," *Technical Leaflet #260*, Nashville: American Association of State and Local History, 2012.

4. Walter Crimm, Martha Morris, and Carole Wharton, *Planning Successful Museum Building Projects* (Lanham, MD: AltaMira Press, 2009), 48–50.

5. Morris, "Recent Trends in Exhibition Development," 10.

6. Author interview with Lauren Telchin-Katz, project manager at the National Museum of American History on November 16, 2016.

7. Author interview with Trevor Jones on November 16, 2016.

8. Susan Hodara, "How to Put a Museum Exhibition Together (Hint: Start with Cash)," *New York Times*, August 26, 2016, accessed October 12, 2016, at http://mobile.nytimes.com/2016/08/28/nyregion/how-to-put-a-museum-exhibition-together-hint-start-with-cash.html?_r = 2&referer.

# CREATING THE PROJECT PLAN

This chapter will cover the creation of the project plan, including creating an enabling charter; developing the project team and assigning a project manager; and creating a detailed timeline, budget, implementation schedule, and evaluation metrics. All of these components are critical elements of project management systems and require disciplined effort. Although these are standard components of the project plan and its implementation, not all museum projects will need this full set of tools. The approach outlined in this chapter most commonly applies to major projects such as exhibitions, collections moves, building renovations or expansions, or substantial database management projects. Small or short-term projects such as special events or an educational program may not need this level of detail. And clearly if the museum has a very small staff they may handle projects in a more informal manner.

## Chartering the Project

Once a project has been approved, as outlined in chapter 5, the museum will formally establish the project and assign key staff to complete the work. A charter is a written document that delineates the scope, schedule, and budget along with the staff assignments for a project. This document describes the end goals and outcomes, assumptions regarding resources and timelines, major stakeholders and accountable managers, team members, a budget, key milestones, and reporting schedules. The charter is a management tool and thus should be approved by the museum's leadership (director or their designate) and distributed to all key staff including functional office heads and project team members. The document may be drafted by a museum committee or more often by the project manager assigned to lead the effort. This stage of the project is formal but important. Without a clear set of expectations, museum projects will flounder. See textbox 6.1 for an example of a museum project charter.

## 6.1.  Sample Project Charter

PROJECT CHARTER: The Best Exhibition Ever

Approved by: Museum Director
Date:

Goals: This exhibition responds to the museum's strategic goal of producing outstanding exhibitions on the topic of community history. The exhibition will draw on scholarship and museum collections representing new areas of collecting responding to changing demographics.

Assumptions: The exhibition will be completed within twelve months using 75 percent museum collections and outside loans, at least three interactives, and working with recent audience evaluation data to assure a responsive educational offering. The temporary exhibitions gallery of 2,500 square feet will be available four weeks in advance of opening. A small brochure, twenty-five-page catalog, four lectures, a symposium, a web page, and five family programs will accompany the museum.

Core Team Members:

Project Manager
Project Director
Curator
Collections Manager
Designer
Educator

Budget: Not to exceed $100,000 (a combination of museum funds and matching grants).

## Developing a Team

The museum's project team may be composed of full- or part-time staff or contractors. Often volunteers and interns play a role as well. The team itself includes the specialists needed to complete the project. For example, a collections move team typically will include curators, registrars, object handlers, conservators, and shippers. An exhibition team will include educators, designers, collections managers, curators, and technology staff. In small museums projects, a few staff members will handle assignments, perhaps with outside consultants, or more often, volunteers. Given all the money in the world, some projects can be populated by dedicated full-time team members. In reality, though, the museum must work with existing staff. In larger museums there may be several teams at work on a variety of projects. Sometimes the same staff member is asked to serve on multiple projects if they are the most experienced individuals.

In most cases the project manager is responsible for building the team. Maintaining a roster of skilled individuals will help in the process of selecting team members. Customarily the project manager will be required to negotiate for the time of the individual team member with their supervisor. This often can be a tricky task if the individual is needed for a variety of priority tasks. In such situations the managers may have to make adjustments to schedules to assure the right person serves on the team. Alternatively, the museum can contract for the needed service or hire a temporary worker. Museums are wise to consider training existing staff in new skills that that could be applied to projects. In considering team qualifications, a mix of skills is best, including interpersonal relations. This mix will be explored in more detail in chapter 7.

In surveys I conducted, it was customary to find cross-functional teams formed at an early stage in the process. Each team member represented his or her functional office reporting back on the development of the project. The project team was composed of a core group and an extended group.[1] This model continues to be a sound approach. The core team includes the key skilled staff that will work together on a regular basis to plan and execute the project. In the case of an exhibition, the core team will customarily include curators, designers, educators, and collections managers. The extended team represents staff that needs to join in the project at specific times, such as when the marketing staff builds a campaign for a new exhibition. Extended team members may be involved in committee reviews, fund-raising support, interactive technology, contractual and legal reviews, and compliance with building codes and accessibility or safety issues. In some cases, individuals will be rotated onto the team for a period of time, particularly if their expertise is critical during that phase of the project. Roles and responsibilities of core and extended team members should be outlined in the project charter.

## Task Analysis and Timelines

The tasks associated with a project can be numerous. In this phase the project manager and team must outline all the major and minor tasks to achieve the end goal. Just as one might outline a written report or thesis, the project task analysis has a set of major elements, and within each heading lay subtasks. In classic project management, the Gantt chart is the format that best pictures the tasks over time. In figure 6.1 you see an example of a simple exhibition project timeline. Most timelines for exhibitions will have many elements, such as predesign (defining the problem and end goals), research on collections, conceptual design with broad sketches of the exhibition, schematic design with elevations and

| Task Name | | Q4 | | | Q1 | | | Q2 | |
|---|---|---|---|---|---|---|---|---|---|
| | Oct | Nov | Dec | Jan | Feb | Mar | Apr | May | Jun |
| 1 Research Topic | | Curator | | | | | | | |
| 2 Develop Concept | | | Curator and Designer | | | | | | |
| 3 Secure Objects | | | | Collections Manager | | | | | |
| 4 Detailed Design | | | Designer | | | | | | |
| 5 Conserve objects | | | | Conservator | | | | | |
| 6 Marketing | | | | | | | Marketing manager | | |
| 7 Fundraising | | | | Development officer | | | | | |
| 8 Website | | | | | | Marketing manager | | | |
| 9 Prepare Space | | | | | Facilities staff | | | | |
| 10 Installation | | | | | | | Exhibits staff | | |
| 11 design education program | | | | | Educator | | | | |
| 12 opening events | | | | | | | Events staff | | |
| 13 public programs | | | | | | | | Education | |

**Figure 6.1. Exhibition Project Gantt Chart. Courtesy of the author.**

more specific information about topics, objects placement, and testing themes with visitors, through to final design documents and hard costs leading to construction. Among these tasks are subtasks associated with object selection, loan negotiation, catalog research, conservation, script writing, web design, fund-raising, and opening events. The basic tasks make up the critical path or steps necessary over time to opening. Typically for each task listed in the chart there can be associated a responsible staff member, a space, a budget line item, time to completion, and due dates. The project manager and the core team complete the final schedule.

The task list and scheduled milestones need to take into consideration a sequence. All tasks are outlined to reflect a logical progress over time. Precedents and dependencies are outlined in the schedule. For example, research on collections will precede design and scriptwriting activities. Conservation treatment will come before object installation. Milestones will mark the completion of a phase of implementation, such as final design. Although there is logic to the creation of task lists, sequences, and milestones, there may be external factors that can create problems. For example, although it is clear how much time might be needed to assemble objects for the exhibition, including obtaining loans, there are always unexpected setbacks. Weather events, staff emergencies, or even cash flow problems might create a delay. Thus, all project schedules should be developed with contingencies built in. Slack time will allow some leeway in meeting milestones. However, some schedules are less flexible, such as when a firm, fixed date has been set for a project's completion. In fact, most projects do have an estimated end date and the schedule is often built "backward" from that date. Where it seems that a task will be compromised or impossible to achieve, the project team will need to make adjustments. Those might be cutting out a portion of the exhibition or adding more resources to assure that they can meet the goal. Budgets often will need to increase or more staff will be added to the project team. The reality is that schedules are in constant flux and need to be frequently updated.

## Critical Path Analysis

Customarily all projects require a critical path. This comprises all the actions that must take place, the time of each task, and their sequence. In the project management discipline this process is considered a powerful method to determine:

- what tasks must be carried out.

- where parallel activity can be performed.

- the shortest time in which you can complete a project.

- the resources needed to execute a project.

- the sequence of activities, scheduling, and timings involved.

- task priorities.

- the most efficient way of shortening time on urgent projects.

Thus an effective critical path analysis can make the difference between success and failure on complex projects. For museum exhibitions a simple critical path would include the sequence of steps and number of days from conceptual design, to object selection and conservation, to script completion, installation, and final opening. Along the way are other steps that may affect the project but will not alter its completion. This analysis can be very useful for assessing the importance of problems faced during the implementation of the plan. Clearly if resources are short and expectations for success are high, this phase of planning is important. A variant of critical path analysis that takes a more skeptical view of the time needed to complete each project stage is PERT, which stands for Program Evaluation and Review Technique. The US Navy developed this technique in the 1950s. The approach includes creating variations on the critical path with estimates of the likelihood of reliability and accuracy in each task completion. It is unlikely that most museum projects will be as complex as building submarines, and thus only a construction firm and other technical consultants under contract in a major building project would probably use PERT analysis.[2]

In considering these approaches to creating schedules, it is imperative to use software that can create reliable project plans, including providing the critical path analysis mentioned above. Many products exist that are highly detailed and sophisticated, such as Microsoft Project. This would work best for projects that include many players, parallel subprojects, and changes in design and available resources over a period of many months or years. However, for most projects, simpler systems exist that allow for ease in sharing information and making decisions, including Smartsheet, Basecamp, Asana, Trello, and Evernote. For creating simple project bar charts, one can use Microsoft Excel, Fast Track, or download free software from the Internet. In any case, the use of automated tools is strongly recommended. These allow for quick updates and sharing information with project team members and others in the museum.

## Budget and Resource Analysis

The allocation of resources usually equates to money. However, equally important resources are staff, collections, facilities, and time. The development of costs associated with all resources (e.g., number of days a staff member may work on a project, or other "overhead" contributions, upgrades to facilities, or collections preparation) is important. Developing accurate budgets begins with examining costs from past projects or comparing numbers from similar projects at other museums. Seeking current costs from outside vendors for the project is important to assure that the budget is not off base. Competitive bids are mandatory in many organizations to assure a fair price. In the case of a major project such as a building renovation, an outside cost estimator may be needed to assure accuracy. Budgets include direct and indirect costs. For an exhibition project, direct costs include all out-of-pocket expenses, including hiring consultants or temporary staff, space preparation, construction of exhibition cases, conservation treatments, photography, web design, shipping and receiving, catalog design, collections acquisition, graphic production, opening parties, and many other items! Indirect costs can include the percentage of the registrar's salary applied to a project, utility and security costs, and administrative services such as accounting, procurement, and human resources. A budget template is a helpful tool in completing this important phase of project planning.[3] Project cost categories are developed to match the museum's accounting systems but can also be translated into reports that will serve to inform stakeholders, such as granting agencies or the museum's board. The budget allows the museum to move forward with active fund-raising, although this has likely already begun at the point the project was approved by management. Early budget estimates are needed to assure that the project is feasible (see textbox 6.2).

The project manager will develop the budget and be responsible for cost controls. Budget line items will be a part of the project schedule. This is important to assure that as the project is implemented sufficient cash is on hand to complete the work. Contractors and vendors expect regular payments. Usually the budget is developed in collaboration with the project team, relying on the experience of department specialists in estimating segments of the work. In fact, some museums will allocate project funds directly to a department for spending. This works well only if the project manager can play a role in monitoring those expenditures. Should insufficient funds materialize for a project, or if the estimates are not realistic, the museum management will need to seek emergency funds, negotiate a loan, or make adjustments to the scope of the project. A worst-case scenario might be cancellation of the project altogether. To avoid that possibility, it is imperative to have a contingency amount built in to the budget.

---

## 6.2. Sample Project Budget

Salaries and Benefits
    Curator                      25,000 (50% of annual salary)
    Educator                   15,000 (30% of annual salary)
Contractual Services
    Designer                   10,000
    Production firm        20,000
    Object conservation    5,000
    Loans (shipping, ins.)   10,000
    Web exhibit           3,000
    Outreach guides      1,500
Miscellaneous Expenses
    Supplies, equipment   5,000
Marketing                  3,000
Opening event/festival    5,000
Contingency (10%)       10,250

**TOTAL Cost**           **$112,750**

Customarily this might be 10 percent of the total, but it varies depending on the complexity of the project. At the outset, a large contingency makes the most sense. For a construction project, the museum may set aside up to 25 percent as a cushion against unforeseen costs. If a project is taking place over a long period of time (e.g., years not months), then escalation factors associated with rising costs must be built into the budget. Another factor to consider is the post-project costs. For example, once the exhibition has opened, what funds are needed to keep it clean, rotate collections, produce new educational products, and make repairs or other updates? With large capital projects such as building expansions, the cost of on-going operations is often covered by endowment funds earmarked for these expenses.

### Funding the Project

Funding projects involves a variety of sources. This can include individual gifts, grants, endowment payout, earned revenue, government appropriations, or financing (loans). Seeking outside funding is mandatory in many museums today, and external funders will expect to see sound and realistic budgets. Some museums have annual operating funds that are allocated to projects such as exhibitions, educational programs, or special events. In some cases, an unrestricted reserve fund may be tapped for an important project. More frequently, money needs to be raised from a variety of sources. These most often include individual gifts, which can be for general operations or more frequently earmarked for a project. Possibly the gift will support only a portion of the project, such as the educational materials for schools. Frequently the museum seeks individual gifts from museum board members or long-term donors. Other sources of funding can come from appropriated funds from government agencies. An example might be the federal government contribution of $250 million to construct the National Museum of African American History and Culture in Washington, D.C. Or another example is Denver, Colorado's $30 million bond initiative that supported the construction of a new collections and education wing at the Museum of Nature and Science. These types of funds are unique and the result of a good deal of planning and advocacy on the part of the museum board and staff. Other fund-raising can be the result of applications to corporations or foundations for grants.

Corporations generally see their support as a means of building brand awareness as good citizens. Foundation grants usually require a long lead time and are often restricted to specific types of uses that match their giving philosophy. For example, the Pew Foundation support of the conservation of the Smithsonian's Star-Spangled Banner flag was a special initiative related to saving America's treasures. In the modern networked world, the rise of Internet-based funding is another important source. Individuals can donate to museums through online portals. The rise of crowdfunding is another option. Kickstarter and various online funding programs are being implemented by museums as they can generate interest in the project as well as build new memberships and audiences. The National Air and Space Museum was able to quickly raise over $700,000 through a Kickstarter campaign to support conservation of Neil Armstrong's space suit.[4] Other ways to raise funds include capital campaigns for large-scale projects or borrowing from local banks to provide a bridge loan against future fund-raising. Often museums may allow a project to proceed with a certain percentage of the money in hand or pledged with the expectation of being able to raise the balance needed. Clearly the museum's risk tolerance will dictate what approach is best. The fund-raising function is the responsibility of the development staff, but in most cases the project manager and key team members will be needed to solicit funds or in-kind services.

## Project Implementation

The project is approved, the charter signed off on, the team formed, the schedule and budget developed. The plan is a go, and progress is under-way. What's next? The project manager will be responsible for monitoring progress as the tasks unfold. Early on an organizing meeting should kick off the project. This is a key opportunity to include management's expectations and introduce the official charter. Over the life of the project, team meetings and management reports are used to coordinate work and monitor progress. No project plan is perfect, and changes are often needed. What about delays? When the budget needs to be adjusted (and it will!), who needs to be involved? Which critical path milestones need to be shared with the board? When does the project manager need to seek help when problems arise? Regular reporting to management or the board can be built into the project schedule. Exceptions to this will be at the discretion of the project manager and team and dictated by their best judgment in most cases. One action that may occur is that of resource leveling. In this case the resources allocated may need adjustments. In museums with multiple projects, there can be a shortage of staff time or money. Resource leveling then involves adjustments that might include adding more staff to a priority project, raising more money for that project, or lengthening the timeline with a later opening date, for example.

Projects can benefit from new approaches in the field. Agile Project Management is being adopted more frequently in the development of technology applications and exhibitions.[5] The basic idea is to create projects in an iterative manner. Self-directed teams who consistently test their ideas with the client develop small pieces of the project. In the case of an exhibition, this process might involve creating and testing design ideas or label text with audiences or with project team members. The feedback from the audience is then considered in the next phase of development. This process allows for constant adjustments, learning among the team members, and presumably a more successful project. In fact, the need for agility in project development was recognized early on by museum director Ron Chew writing in *Museum News*, where he stated that a "quick response model makes the most sense." Moving away from methodical development practices to small teams developing imaginative responses to critical social issues was the model at Wing Luk Museum in Seattle. Chew pioneered working with nonspecialists and community members to respond to their issues and concerns. Experimentation was an opportunity for learning, keeping the best practices and rejecting ideas that did not work out.[6]

## Evaluation Metrics

Although evaluation is an activity that usually occurs after the project is completed, the measures needed to judge its success or failure need to be defined at the outset. Very few projects by granting agencies or foundations without a sound evaluation plan in place will be funded. These plans need to consider the strategic goals of the museum, the way that the specific project links to those goals, and the methods of assessing the outcomes. These are most often defined in terms of visitor experience, public response, and overall quality. Other measures that can be included in an evaluation plan will be cost variances, team performance, on-time delivery, and adherence to museum mission, vision, and values. These internal and external measures can be developed in terms of numbers (e.g., how often the website was accessed, how quickly money was raised, how many positive press reviews were generated) or in terms of quality (e.g., the learning outcomes of a particular exhibition, the new research generated, the accessibility of the programs for underserved audiences, or the lessons learned about project team dynamics). Other types of measures used by museums to assess program success are usually attendance, increases in funding, press coverage, and membership numbers. Chapter 9 will examine the evaluation systems for projects in more detail.

## Management Issues

The museum needs clear policies and procedures for managing projects. These can include how projects are chartered, the committees involved in decision making and ongoing review, and policies on budgeting and fundraising. Surveys show that many museums have developed documentation on how to create exhibitions largely to determine the roles and responsibilities of departments and guidelines for decision making. After many years of detailed policy and procedure development, museums should create streamlined guidelines including checklists for stepping through the process. Often this occurs as a result of lessons learned in the evaluation phase. The National Museum of the American Indian produced their Project Management Guidelines document in 2000. This effort to formalize the process of project review, chartering, and implementation details the roles and responsibilities of both team members and functional offices along with senior management. Since then the museum has continued to refine their process with a central planning office. Christa Stabler is head of the Executive Planning Office of the National Museum of the American Indian. She has worked at the museum off and on since 2000 in varying roles including public programs, exhibitions, and on the transition team to the new museum opening in 2004. Stabler spent about ten years at a small community museum in Virginia leading operations, expansion, and finance. The Executive Planning office is responsible for managing projects, mainly exhibitions, with three full-time project managers on staff. She states, "The project managers in the Executive Planning Office are primarily on exhibitions in D.C. and New York. We have also overseen large loans, grants, wayfinding, and AV programs. A Project Manager is typically assigned when there are large amounts of resources involved, or if a project has multiple stakeholders and needs to be organized and vetted for senior management decision making." The project managers do not have formal training in project management theory but are experienced museum professionals. The Smithsonian network of project managers is a great resource for these staff who share best practices.

Projects are evaluated in a postmortem analysis. As Stabler noted, "At these points we address lessons learned, financial success, marketing, and a pain/gain matrix. Where I am looking for us to make improvements is in how and when we identify the applicability of lessons learned in ongoing projects. Databases are tricky because they may not be able to help the Project Manager in real time, or need to be very specific in how the lessons are tagged to be relatable to any search. With more of our senior management moving on in the next few years, it is important that we work to capture some institutional memory, and develop a practical way to reference it later."

Stabler notes that there is a review and approval process in place, but that flexibility is important to the process. "With so many various factors, the course of a project could change at any given time. This is where the skill and resourcefulness of each Project Manager is important. The relationships built, the strength of the larger team, and the ability to be a problem solver for the common good all come in to play." She goes on to note that many individuals play a role in a project's success, including office heads and senior managers. It is not unusual to need to adjust resources to meet challenges.[7]

As is the practice at NMAI, best practices include a central office or individual responsible for project oversight in museums that have multiple projects underway. Often this role is assigned to the director of exhibitions or the chief operating officer. This role is critical for assuring that projects do not compete with each other for budget, space, or staff. Despite having policies and senior management oversight, a variety of problems can arise in the planning and implementation of projects. The more critical issues are outlined below.

*Standardized costs.* Developing realistic budgets requires close attention to the cost-estimating process. In very large projects museums can hire cost estimators to work with their plans in order to assure that they have a reliable estimate, such as with an expansion project. However, in most cases the project manager will need to rely on prior project costs for similar activities (e.g., graphic design or exhibition case construction). Maintaining a database of cost histories is invaluable. This is particularly important in the feasibility phase when straw budgets are developed for decision making. Often benchmarking comparisons of other museums' costs is a good source of information. Working with financial staff is important particularly when there is a need to include overhead costs in the process of grant writing. Board members might ask about cost per square foot for exhibitions or costs per object for a collection move. These numbers can vary widely, so caution should prevail in sharing them without explaining they are only estimates.

*Life cycle costing.* A relatively new area of budgeting and planning, life cycle costing takes into consideration that some exhibitions or other projects may be long term and need updating along with daily maintenance. Using a budget template provides an opportunity to build in long-term costs at the outset of an exhibition. For example, daily maintenance, object rotation, periodic updates, and other costs will assure a fresh exhibition for the public. Building systems also are subject to long-term maintenance and upgrades. Commissioning of a new building's infrastructure systems can assure investments are calculated for the life of the facility.

*Cash flow.* Linking incoming funds and outgoing expenses requires a close look at cash flow. Forecasting the flow for major milestones and for promised payment dates can avoid problems in the future. Income should always be sufficient to cover obligations. Where there are gaps, the museum will need to redirect funds from other sources or borrow money in the form of a bridge loan. Understanding the cash flow needs is critical to negotiating donations and setting up a system of pledge payments.

*Balanced planning.* Many museums will proceed with multiple projects whether long term or short in duration. The museum should maintain a master calendar of all approved projects in order to assure that the organization is not overcommitted. The senior management serves as a capacity gauge for the museum's work. Sometimes the project has been poorly defined and there may be need to redesign or scale back due to cost overruns. Be alert to situations in which projects fall behind or staff is overcommitted and stressed out. Assigning a senior staff member to monitor all projects can be of great value so that adjustments can be made to avoid disasters.

*Individual accountability.* Often there are difficulties with staff meeting deadlines and understanding the expectations of working in the team environment. Developing performance standards, establishing a regular meeting schedule, and empowering project managers will alleviate this problem. Often staff does not have training in project management systems, and this is something the museum's leadership should provide. An established program of introducing staff to the basics of project accountability helps. The elements of teambuilding, internal communications, dealing with conflicts, and building museumwide buy-in to projects will be discussed in further detail in chapters 7 and 8.

*Unexpected roadblocks.* Despite excellent planning and confidence in project implementation, there are always setbacks. Environmental disasters, loss of key staff, public criticism, or other unplanned-for events are not uncommon. Consider the impact of federal government shutdowns or hiring freezes on the plans of museums at the Smithsonian or National Park Service for any number of critical projects. External stakeholders such as community members, the press, or government agencies may have an interest in the museum's programs. A new secretary at the Smithsonian solicited a major gift for the Museum of American History in 2001 that led to reassignment of staff to managing the donor's concerns for many months. This disruption created significant morale issues among staff members and delayed work on other priority projects. On a brighter note, your museum could receive unexpected funds for a key part of the project implementation. For example, a corporate sponsor might offer a major gift for a website or programs for underserved audiences. These may not have been in the original scope or budget. Assuming no strings are attached, the museum will need to add these activities to the timeline and redirect staff to oversee development of the new components of the project. Here is where the agile project team can shine. In chapter 7 the work of teams will be examined in greater detail.

## Discussion Questions

1. Does your museum have a formal project management program? Are project charters, milestone reviews, and resource leveling actions in place?
2. What project management software is best for a small museum?
3. How do you link the project budget to annual operations if the project will extend over one or more fiscal years?

## Notes

1. Kathleen Fleming, "Exhibit Research Project: Trends in Exhibition Process and Planning," an unpublished benchmarking study conducted for the Office of the Deputy Director, National Museum of American History, June 1997.

2. Critical Path Analysis and PERT Charts, accessed at Mindtools.com, October 15, 2016, https://www.mindtools.com/critpath.html.

3. Martha Morris, "Developing an Exhibition Budget Template," in *Manual of Museum Exhibitions*, edited by Gail Lord and Barry Lord (Lanham, MD: AltaMira Press, 2002), 317.

4. Marina Koren, "The Smithsonian Raises $700,000 on Kickstarter to Save Neil Armstrong's Spacesuit," *The Atlantic*, August 18, 2015, accessed October 30, 2016, at http://www.theatlantic.com/technology/archive/2015/08/smithson ian-neil-armstrong-spacesuit-museum/401663/.

5. Mindtools.com, "Agile Project Management: Organizing Flexible Projects," accessed October 16, 2016, at https://www.mindtools.com/pages/article/ agile-project-management.htm. An example of using the Agile approach was described in the archives of the Museums and the Web conference in 2008. The article featured the work of a team of museum professionals in creating a software system for social tagging called steve.com. The team worked on their project in small chunks, interspersed with user testing and cycles of development in response to user feedback. See D. Ellis, M. Jenkins, W. Lee, and R. Stein, "Agile Methods for Project Management," accessed January 7, 2017, at http://www .museumsandtheweb.com/biblio/agile_methods_project_management.html.

6. Ron Chew, "Toward a More Agile Model of Exhibition-Making," *Museum News*, November/December 2000, 47–48.

7. *Project Management Guidelines*, 2000, National Museum of the American Indian, unpublished manuscript, shared with author during benchmarking surveys of museum approaches to project management 2000; and author email exchange with Christa Stabler, January 25, 2017.

# CREATING THE PROJECT TEAM

## Why Teams?

The project team is the heart of the successful project. Negotiating the feasibility study and decision process, chartering the project, and building the schedule and budget all rely on individuals committed to collaborative work. Teams are necessary for many reasons and have been proven to make all the difference in the execution of museum projects. In studies I and others have conducted it is clear that the team approach is prevalent for both planning and implementation of museum exhibitions and programs. In fact, as was discussed in chapter 2, many museums that have undergone extensive strategic planning and reorganization have adopted a team-based approach to general operations as well as special projects, including the process of strategic planning itself. The value of teams is in greater delegation, improved communication, and, hopefully, faster decision making. The successful team develops ground rules for operations, shares a clear goal or mission, and represents a variety of skills. Also, the value of cross-functional teams is in mutual understanding and team learning, diminishing the silo effect that hampers internal communications.[1]

The University of Missouri Museum Studies department conducted a comprehensive survey of a variety of museums responding to questions about teams. The findings indicated that a team approach was common for exhibition development, most teams were composed of five or more people from different functional offices, and that leadership was vested in senior staff members such as curators and scientists. In the case of museums with budgets over $5 million, there was a dedicated project manager. The survey found that decisions were made based on consensus and that when conflicts arose they were most often about unclear team roles and authority.[2]

The value of teams in the museum is that they can help staff work more creatively, they can educate the staff about the process of project development and decision making, and they allow for key stakeholders to be involved in the earliest phases of project design. A good example would be a team dedicated to moving collections where each member is needed to assure success and each needs to work with the other:

- *conservators* to review objects' physical needs

- *registrars* to verify legal status and object description

- *curators* to determine which objects are needed in what locations (storage, exhibits, loans)

- *art handlers and shipping specialists* to package and transport the objects

Understanding the nature of teams is often problematic. While some teams are formed for a specific project, such as a task force making recommendations for new collecting areas, other teams are long term, such as a standing committee that reviews and approves exhibition ideas. One person is either appointed or elected to lead a team in some instances, while in others the leadership rotates. In some cases there is a self-managed team with no clear leader. The latter team members work without top-down direction, in a consensus-driven mode, with exceptional levels of communication. No matter what model, successful teams are characterized by:

- a strong sense of *mutual accountability* and respect for each other

- *roles and responsibilities* that are clear

- the *success* of the project that is *shared* by all

- *collective work products*

- *shared leadership*

These teams are formed through the direction of higher management to achieve a particular objective, but this is restated by the team and clarified and translated into specific goals and tasks and a common approach.

Therefore, working together improves communication, creativity, and efficiency. Effective teams also have distinctive characteristics, including:

- they are *small* (under ten people)
- they have a *mix of skills* and learning styles
- they are trained in problem solving and decision making
- they are open, risk taking, and supportive
- they receive encouragement, positive feedback, and recognition
- they celebrate small wins
- they often work in a common space

The above qualities reflect the research of Katzenbach and Smith, who studied high-performing teams in businesses and nonprofits.[3] They found that the most successful teams are driven by well-defined outcomes and expected results. These teams do not depend on the leader as a central catalyst as much as the team as a whole and its operating ethic. This works only with a disciplined approach to the team process. A genuine mutual concern and respect is shared among members. Research also points to the importance of integrating team performance with individual learning. Team members learn about themselves, their colleagues, and gain new skills. As we examine the case studies of successful museum teams, we will explore these factors. Do they operate in a high-performing manner? One of the first challenges museums may face is finding the skills needed to build the team from among their own staff and assuring they are trained in collaboration and problem solving.

## Options for Organizing the Team

Team organization will vary depending on the size and complexity of the project or the working culture of the museum itself. Some group members working on a project operate in a more independent manner, completing their portion of the work to be handed over to another individual. This is likely to be the case in smaller organizations with a few projects. On the opposite end of this approach would be the dedicated project team where all members work exclusively on the project to meet a high-profile deadline. Developing a major traveling exhibition could use this type of approach. Curators, designers, educators, and collections staff are assigned to work full time on a high-priority effort. Most museum projects will fall within the "matrix" model where staff are assigned part time to work with a project manager (see chapter 3).

The matrix is a practical approach, although it brings with it ambiguity and often high levels of stress for the staff member. Dual-reporting relationships (to both the project manager and the functional supervisor) can lead to misunderstandings and conflicts. In this approach, museum management should be attuned to the need for adjusting the allocation of staff time across projects, anticipating conflicts, and adding more resources or adjusting the timeline for projects. In addition, the project manager and functional manager should work closely to define performance expectations for the assigned team member. Beyond this time management issue is the tension that may exist between function and project. A more bureaucratic organization that relies on a hierarchy of decision making will be less likely to survive in a matrix approach than a museum that is clearly willing and able to be flexible in a turbulent, changing environment. A matrix-based team will also be subject to potential turnover, as staff may need to be reassigned. Every time a new player is added the project is in danger of being derailed or redefined under the influence of new members. The inefficiencies of structures in projects are also exacerbated by poor information systems and communications flow. It is not uncommon for misunderstandings and garbled messages to occur in our fast-paced environment. The more people that are involved in sharing information the greater the risk of misunderstandings or omissions. There is value then in looking at differing types of structures for project teams. J. Davidson Frame, an expert on project management in organizations, outlines a number of structures that might be useful depending on complexity and size of the project.

The *surgical team* employs a central technical leader with many special assistants. The assistants are specialists, but their work is defined by the "surgeon." The technical lead needs to be highly knowledgeable and skilled to assure top quality in meeting project goals. An example of this might be a conservator with specialized training working on a highly valuable artifact assisted by technicians who help to prepare treatment materials, photograph the object, or manage other documentation of the project.

*The isomorphic team* is one in which the segments of the project each have corresponding responsible team members. For example, compiling a grant application may involve a team that divides the work into research, project goals, budget, and evaluation. Each section is independently developed and should move with some speed to completion. What doesn't work about this model is the lack of team integration. This then falls to the project manager to coordinate the final document. This approach is very much the opposite of the *egoless team.* Here there is no obvious leader and decisions are reached through consensus. Often this is a small, creative group, perhaps with no more than three or four members. With no appointed leader the team members work equally but must spend considerable time in communications. Turnover in this team would not be a good option. An example might be a small team working on the early phases of an exhibition concept plan. The more customary approach used in museums especially for exhibition development is a *specialty team* structure. Here the individuals with expertise work on sections of a project such as design, education, or script writing. The individuals work independently, but often team members impact their work. The decision making can often shift from one team member to the other depending on where they are in the timeline.[4]

The use of the team *approach* continues to be of value to many modern organizations. In recent years there has been a growing emphasis on the self-managed (or "egoless") team environment, called "holocracy." These are popular structures that foster innovation, flexibility, and productivity. Structures called "circles" attempt to do away with traditional hierarchy. Staff moves in and out of the circles as needed to complete work. Teams design their work and govern themselves with formal written pledges to detail mutual accountability. Decisions are made by consensus. Staff members may have more than one role in these circles that emphasize a multiskilled workforce. These types of teams form and disband and redefine individual roles in response to the needs of the organization.[5] In fact, some organizations are foregoing permanent staff hiring for the practice of creating "on-demand teams" that are composed of consultants, freelancers, and specialists, often from the millennial and baby boomer workforce. The value of this approach is that the teams draw on skilled experts instead of existing staff that may not be trained for the specialized work. This allows the organization to move quickly in a competitive world and ideally save money on ongoing employee overhead costs. As was discussed in chapter 3, the contemporary workforce is changing, and recent surveys show that individuals might prefer this "on-demand" type of work experience over permanent employment.[6] Would this work for museums? Perhaps only in start-ups or in museums with a mandate to work with intense levels of innovation. In fact, one major criticism of self-managed teams is the lack of coordination, detail development, advocacy, and conflict-resolution skills of a strong project manager. In applying new modes of project work, Google found that employing leaders who develop and motivate their team and share information effectively was important in a culture of highly independent engineers. All these "soft" skills were critical to revising their work structures. And this was reinforced by feedback surveys from employees.[7]

Sometimes the best decision making about program goals is done in a very informal setting. Lunchroom meetings were a favorite location of a self-managed team at the Museum of American History in the 1990s. Motivated by a common interest in the history of workers and managers, this self-selected group of staff met informally to develop ideas. Lunchroom discussions led them to create projects around exhibitions, collecting, and program development. This self-managed team gradually created viable ideas that management was able to resource. The team had no appointed leader but worked collaboratively with a lot of communications. Roles of the team shifted depending on the product at hand (collecting, exhibition research, writing). Given the topic of their work, this open process and shared authority was most appropriate.

## Forming Museum Teams

In the case of a major museum project, such as a renovation, new building, or institutional strategic plan, the team process can be complex. At the outset, the museum will need to form a high-level steering committee composed of the executive director, board members, and other senior staff such as exhibition programs, finance, and fund-raising. This team sets policy, oversees project development, and provides an interface to outside stakeholders. Such large endeavors will require an overall project manager who will oversee the work of all the major players such as construction contractors, consultants, and the existing staff. Other working groups or teams will be created to develop specific functions required to complete a new building, such as collections storage, visitor experience/exhibitions, facilities operations, and development and marketing. Small projects may never need this level of organization. In fact, the museum may choose to appoint the most knowledgeable staff member to run the project. If it's an exhibition, the curator may be selected as the team leader while other staff, volunteers, or contractors are brought in to assist. In an ideal scenario a team of specialists including a curator, designer, educator, and others work together from the outset to define the themes, design, and core public programs. In the case of any project in the museum—large or small—one person should be appointed to advocate for the project and the team.

Determining what skills are needed for a project is the first step. Maintaining an inventory of skilled staff can be helpful as teams are formed. For major projects, a mix of permanent staff, contractors, volunteers, and new hires is not unusual. Some existing staff might be assigned to a project and given specialized training instead of outsourcing the function. In museums with limited staff, a program of cross-training can provide the variety of skills that can be deployed, not unlike the holocracy approach described above. Typical team members for an exhibition would include curators, registrars, educators, designers, publications specialists, and community advocates. For a collections digitization project, the museum will need curators, registrars, photographers, and technology staff to design the database and manage the rapid-capture photography systems. In addition to this mix of skills the high-performing team should consider a mix of learning styles. The learning styles refer to various preferences of individuals in regard to communications and interpersonal relations. These will be examined in more detail in chapter 8.

## Resistance to the Team Process

One unexpected reaction to forming a team can be a resistance. Katzenbach and Smith observed this as a problem in their research. This stems from the emphasis on individual achievement in our society. There are many reasons for resistance, including personal discomfort with being linked with other individuals, threats to feelings of self-worth, or feeling that teamwork will impact their status and performance rating.[8] The types of complaints that may arise include the fact that teams waste time in meetings, working on one's own is more efficient, group consensus can reduce the quality of the final project, team members will not respect each other's ideas, and teams spend too much time on process, not products. Despite these attitudes, most museums find that the team working together helps staff understand why and how project decisions are made as well as to learn about the broader picture of museum operations, as was described in Senge's "learning organization" concepts featured in chapter 4.

Team performance is dependent on a strong early phase. A kickoff or orientation meeting is critical. This is an opportunity to do the following:

- introduce the project charter and roles

- clarify the project scope and expectations

- develop a meeting schedule

Beyond this initial meeting, there is a need to build a trusting relationship through informal sessions, lunches, or retreats. The team will need to set ground rules for operations and decision making, as well as examine their understanding of the end goals and the key milestones in the project plan. Budgets and other resources will need to be reviewed and updated. Members of the team will need to have written performance objectives reflecting their personal accountability. The role of functional managers may also need to be outlined. For example, a collections manager on a move team may need to get approval from their supervisor for any deviation in the museum's collections management policy.

As discussed in chapter 6, museums often use distinct core and extended teams (see figure 7.1). The core team spends significant amounts of time on the project (for exhibits it would be curatorial content, collections management, exhibition design, and educational programs), while the extended team is composed of functional staff that moves in and out depending on the need for their input, such as development, finance, or human resources staff. For most projects the responsibilities of team members reflect their functional departments and expected skills. For example, skills needed in developing technology applications include

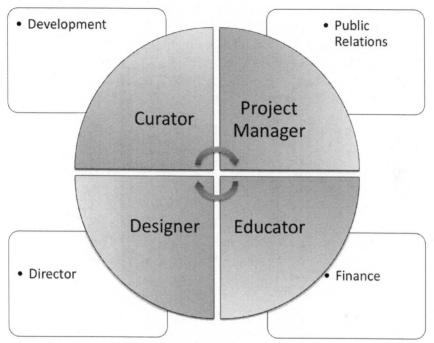

Figure 7.1. Core and extended team. Courtesy of the author.

script and storyline, educational outcomes, collections data, and possibly audience targets. A capital campaign will require prospect researchers, social media specialists, graphic designers, and fund-raisers.

For some teams there can be more than one leadership role, including a project director and a project manager. The project director or sponsor serves as the keeper of the vision for the project, advocates with external parties, and makes key decisions. A project manager may then be responsible for schedules, team assignments, budgets, resources allocations, and team training or counseling. Depending on the type of museum, there may be a lead exhibition developer or an audience advocate or evaluator. The former develops the content, and the latter contributes to the testing of and interpretation of the success of concept designs and scripts with visitors.[9] In some museums external advisors are invited to join the team; for example, museums may seek the views and guidance of an outside community curator.

One helpful way to describe roles and responsibilities is to develop a Responsibility Chart. This allows for a more detailed look at who has ultimate authority and how relationships interact (see table 7.1).

In this chart the functions or responsibilities are labeled in such a way that it is clear who does what for each activity in the project. Clearly these roles can vary among museums, and there is no standard assumed in this example. The use of the chart is a tool that can help to avoid confusion among the varied players in the project. Not shown here is the role of functional managers such as assistant directors or other office heads who are not a part of the team but contribute their staff to the effort. Surely there will be some activities that need to be approved by senior managers, and these should also be outlined in the project charter. The role of the functional manager is to assure professional standards and policies, and in the case of project teams it will provide higher-level oversight and advocacy. An example of how this type of chart can be used is the Accountability Chart illustrated in Appendix D.

## The Contractor on the Team

A formal process is needed to solicit the services of outside consultants as contractors for a project. The museum will have rules and policies that cover this process, but it is important to be very clear in the solicitation to describe the nature of the work, the qualifications of the contractor, the timeframe, and cost parameters. Contractors have specialized skills that will add significantly to the quality of the project. In many museum situations, an existing staff member must manage a contractor. For example, the registrar serves to coordinate the work of packing and shipping contractors, or a design manager serves as a liaison to the exhibition design firm. In fact, the contractor may be an individual or a firm. Aside from

**Table 7.1. Responsibility Chart**

|  | Script | Loans | Budget |
|---|---|---|---|
| Project Manager | C | C | R |
| Curator | R | A | C |
| Registrar | C | R | C |
| Director | A | I | A |

R = Responsible A = Approve C = Consult I = Inform

the legal requirement that contractors operate independently and cannot be treated as employees, there are problems of integration with the team. Contractors are short-term members of the team; they may have little knowledge of the museum's mission and operating values, and may not feel a sense of loyalty to the project team. Sometimes they are highly sought-after experts who have a big reputation and may tend to push the museum staff to accept their ideas instead of contributing to a team effort. The process of selecting a contractor is often lengthy and bureaucratic as matching the needs of the museum with the skills and experience of an outside firm requires very detailed negotiations. A case study on the Smithsonian's major exhibition on transportation *America on the Move* points to the reality of hiring outside design and construction service firms who may do the more creative planning work while existing staff end up in a management relationship with them. In fact, many museums that have cut staff positions over the years to save money may now have to contract for services that were once done by permanent staff, such as exhibition production or conservation. According to project director Steven Lubar, "A museum that hires many contractors to do its work has different management challenges than a museum that manages the work internally. It needs more contract managers—but contract managers with the skills to understand, oversee, and evaluate technical work." In this case, design, production, and education were contracted out and over twenty-four firms (some subcontractors) played a role.[10] For a museum to be successful working with contractors, the definition of the requirements of the project must be clear and detailed and the qualifications of the contractor closely examined to assure they have the experience and will be able to meet your expectations. This phase of the project is one that needs considerable time and careful assessment.

## The Project Manager or Team Leader's Role

The role of project manager is one that can make or break the success of teams. Much has been written about the unique nature of this position, which is part manager and part leader. This is not a purely supervisory or coordinating position on the team, but one that brings together the resources allocated to produce the desired product within time, on budget, and with a sense of celebration on the part of all involved. As discussed earlier, not every museum has dedicated project managers. Often the work is assigned to a functional staff member who has the most knowledge about the work. That individual will still need to play a coordinating role among peers and others. So no matter what the title, the skills are often the same. In very large projects such as an expansion or renovation, it is not unusual to hire an outside expert to run the project. The downside of this decision might be their lack of understanding of the museum business and even a lack of dedication to the mission and values of the museum. The selection of a project manager for large and complex initiatives requires a good deal of consideration. For example, a museum may appoint a senior staff member to oversee the development and implementation of a renovation or new building. Or perhaps they will select a seasoned consultant to join the museum to help them through the project. When the museum is not experienced with construction work or has many other priorities, an outside firm can be hired as an owner's representative. In either case, the level of trust in the individual's understanding of the museum's culture and goals is critical.[11]

Project managers are often the ones charged with advocating for the project, the team process, and handling numerous stakeholders with varying work styles and expectations.[12] Team dynamics can be a constant challenge, and it is one aspect of managing projects that requires finesse. One of the most important functions of the project manager is building the team. This requires good working relations with both team members and functional managers. As noted earlier in this chapter, in the matrix environment, project managers negotiate with functional office heads for the time of their staff. There is no authority in this role so that skills of communication and influence are paramount.

There are two main responsibilities for the project manager: administration and leadership. Obviously the administrative role involves securing staff and contract support, building the team, scheduling, budgeting, milestone review, meeting management, reporting on progress, and handling the flow of information among the many individuals invested in the project itself. Project managers have to *know* the business, understand the tasks and costs, and be aware of operating policies and procedures. They may need to hire new staff and negotiate contracts. Monitoring progress involves frequent milestone reviews and formal reporting on the status of the project to senior management and the museum board. They are the corporate memory of the project and manage all documentation. Their leadership function is more complex. It involves building a high-performing team, providing training and positive feedback, monitoring group health, listening to stakeholders, keeping open communications at all levels of the organization, and resolving conflict and solving problems. Clearly these are all difficult tasks, and not everyone is capable of meeting these expectations.

Challenges abound in this role. Poorly identified needs can lead to cost overruns or rework. Poor planning and controls and the inability to influence teams or higher-level management can derail the project. Often project managers are handling two or three major projects at once or running projects plus ongoing functional work. Therefore, savvy project managers need to work with discipline and speed to anticipate problems in advance and get below the surface to examine hidden agendas of team members. Being flexible and risk averse are two perhaps opposing traits. According to J. Davidson Frame, things will go wrong and the project manager needs to know how to work the system through their personal charisma if not formal authority. One-on-one meetings and informal reviews by checking in on the team can be a confidence-building approach. The reality is that the team is a temporary entity, and the project manager has limited authority. Often the project will be assigned a senior management sponsor (say a Vice President for Programs) who will work to assure that the project manager has support at a higher level when needed. However, the power of the project manager should emanate from their ability to influence the team through trust building, helping them resolve time management or technical problems, and providing positive feedback and recognition. A high level of maturity and sensitivity to individual concerns is important along with a strong understanding of the museum's values and standards of production.

Frame has designated project management as the "accidental profession" in that many times people are tapped for this job without any formal training. They thus learn on the job and over time may become very proficient. Serving as a conduit between staff and management is also a unique function. They have a great deal of knowledge about the organization and its weaknesses and strengths as they have a unique view of several functions. What lessons they have learned are passed on informally to others in the organization.[13] In conversations with museum project managers, I have learned that the challenges of their assignments require consistent attention to detail, including contract negotiation, budget and timeline adjustments, team meetings, advocacy to senior management for resources, and conflict resolution within the team. Frequently they must meet one on one with functional office managers to resolve problems. Many of these individuals are in the category of Frame's "accidental" managers. They were hired for traditional functional office responsibilities. As highly productive individuals they were given an opportunity to lead, but of course they learned on the job. Working in a large museum brings with it a strong silo mentality. Often projects are actually organized within a functional office with only occasional interaction with other museum units. For example, an active program of public programs that link to the museum mission and special exhibition program can be developed by an events manager who is responsible for venue selection, speakers, schedules, contracts, and registration while relying on other offices to provide marketing and budget support. Another approach involves the work of technology staff in developing a new website for a small museum. Team leadership involves running a series of workshops to design the website and including input from several functional offices including curatorial. Designing a website involves new ways of writing and user-centered design solutions. These approaches can be foreign to traditional curatorial staff and thus involve more diplomacy and team learning than a traditional exhibition, for example.

The role of the project manager in the area of collections management is critically important. An interesting example is that of the J. Paul Getty Museum. As a senior project manager within the Collections Department, Jessica Palmieri plays a critical role in planning and managing important initiatives. Her department is responsible for collections programs that encompass all of the curatorial, conservation, and registrarial staff. Palmieri supports essential functions around the museum's art collections and their development, ensures loans are given institutional oversight, and coordinates museumwide policy updates and projects. The J. Paul Getty Trust (of which the museum is a part) has established a formal project management job family with specific staff assigned to this role across the institution. Like many large museums, this role is one that "manages the development and implementation of projects involving departmental or cross-functional teams. The project manager plans and schedules activities and monitors the work to assure on time and on budget outcomes." As a senior project manager, Palmieri is often responsible for tasks "that do not fall neatly within any other department and/or require someone with a broader institutional purview who is able to see how each of the various constituents can contribute to the completion of various goals while simultaneously being conscientious of keeping multiple agendas moving forward." Her work involves creating appropriate policies and documentation for the work, and her oversight assures a high level of accountability. Special projects that she has led include creating a long-term plan for sustaining the Central Garden designed by artist Robert Irwin. This involves coordinating a team from several departments and external advisors along with the artist himself. Another example of a cross-functional project is the Emergency Preparedness plan and associated museumwide training. In her role she has "agency to move projects forward" and takes initiative to improve the operations of the department. She notes, "So much of project management in the realm of collections seems to come down to common sense, resourcefulness, and people skills, combined with a drive to get things done."[14]

Success in leading projects of all types requires special skills. Most importantly, in conversation with museum staff I heard the words *people skills* as well as *problem solving* and the ability to analyze information to make sound recommendations. Beyond these personal skills, there are options for training in best practices. The Project Management Institute does training worldwide in the basics as well as more sophisticated systems. Responding to the need for improved management skills, the American Association for State and Local History offers a project management workshop series in its continuing education program. Designed from a pilot funded by the IMLS, this program provides both face-to-face seminars and online training. Over four hundred museum staff had been trained between 2009 and 2016.[15] The successful project manager will find that they have unique skills that make them a critical member of the workforce. Those who have completed the certification training offered by the Project Management Institute are able to transfer their talents to a variety of projects. Stephanie Shapiro is a museum professional who has completed formal training in project management. Having first earned PMI's Certified Associate in Project Management

(CAPM®) certification, this helped laid the groundwork for earning the PMI's Project Management Professional (PMP®) certification. The PMP® is relevant across all industries and gives a common nomenclature and foundation for project managers to apply, making the learning curve of industries such as consulting less steep. In her museum work, Shapiro notes, "Working in Advancement Services, the PMP® provided a basis of tools, resources, and processes to apply to each unique project. From initiating to closing projects, the PMP®'s infrastructure allows for a starting-off point. Here, having a common nomenclature and foundation allowed me to successfully execute different types of projects from revamping a business process (such as travel systems); change management; database implementation; launching a new website, and more." Shapiro is a management consultant at Eagle Hill Consulting in Arlington, Virginia. She formerly worked at the Smithsonian Institution Office of Advancement and is cochair of the PIC-Green committee of AAM.[16]

## Discussion Questions

1. Does your museum use project teams for developing exhibitions? If so, do you have a written policy and procedure for forming teams?
2. Given the types of project-organizing structures outlined in this chapter, what works best for a small museum that has an active, changing exhibition program?
3. As a project manager or team leader, how does one deal with the issue of resistance to the team approach?

## Notes

1. Martha Morris, "Recent Trends in Exhibition Development," in *Exhibitionist* 21, no. 1 (2002): 8–12.

2. Jay Rounds and Nancy McIlvaney's 1999 research as reported in the *Exhibitionist* provides an important and comprehensive analysis of the team approach. "Who's Using the Team Process? How's It Going?" *Exhibitionist*, National Association of Museum Exhibitions, 19, no. 1 (2000): 3–18.

3. Jon R. Katzenbach and Douglas K. Smith, *The Wisdom of Teams* (New York: HarperCollins, 2003).

4. J. Davidson Frame, *Managing Projects in Organizations* (San Francisco: Jossey-Bass, 2003), 88–95.

5. Ethan Bernstein, John Bunch, Niko Canner, and Michael Lee, "Beyond the Holacracy Hype," in *Harvard Business Review* 94, no. 7/8 (2016): 39–49.

6. Marty Zwilling, "Build On-Demand Teams Instead of Hiring Employees," *Huffington Post*, accessed October 29, 2016, at http://www.huffingtonpost.com/marty-zwilling/build-on-demand-teams-ins_b_12651756.html.

7. David A. Garvin, "How Google Sold Its Engineers on Management," *Harvard Business Review*, no. 91, December 2013.

8. Katzenbach and Smith, *The Wisdom of Teams*, 20–24.

9. Jennifer Bine, "A Project Manager Is . . ." *Exhibitionist*, National Association of Museum Exhibitions 25, no. 1 (2006): 71–82.

10. Steven Lubar, "The Making of America on the Move," *Curator* 47, no. 1 (January 2004): 40.

11. Walter Crimm, Martha Morris, and L. Carole Wharton, *Planning Successful Museum Building Projects* (Lanham, MD: AltaMira Press, 2009), 43.

12. Polly McKenna-Cress and Janet Kamien, *Creating Exhibitions* (New York: John Wiley and Sons, 2013), 194.

13. Frame, *Managing Projects in Organizations*, 69–70.

14. Author interview of Jessica Palmieri, January–February 2017.

15. Author conversation with Cherie Cook, Senior Program Manager, AASLH, October 26, 2016.

16. Author email exchange with Stephanie Shapiro on January 23, 2017.

## CHAPTER EIGHT
# SUCCESSFUL TEAM DYNAMICS

Chapter 7 provided an introduction to building teams, including their optimal structures and key skills. Clarity in role definition, incorporating outside expertise, and providing project leadership results in successful team experiences. Yet we know that many factors impact the team's ability to achieve their goals without bumps along the way.

The high-performing team as described in chapter 7 is small in number, has a mix of skills, works closely together, and exhibits mutual accountability. Beyond these elements a successful team must also have a mix of learning styles, exceptional communications skills, and flexibility in responding to change. Sophisticated teams develop and employ a methodology for problem solving and conflict resolution. Successful teams experience problems, changes, and internal strife but will be able to overcome these challenges. This chapter will examine the importance of teambuilding and individual learning styles, developing team operating norms, managing and sharing information about projects, developing tools for collaborative decision making, resolving conflicts, and the role of the project manager as an advocate for team success.

Team dysfunctions are not uncommon. In research done by the University of Pennsylvania's Wharton School of Business, the "dark side" of teams occurs when groups become insular and less efficient. Team members become entrenched in their own ideas and values, and after working on consensus-driven decisions, accepting new viewpoints may meet with resistance. Reluctance to include outside information can be destructive as good ideas could easily be rejected. The reasoning behind this reveals the team's desire to protect their cohesion and validate that their ideas are the right ones.[1]

Other problems that arise in the team involve the influence of communities of practice.[2] Each team member represents a professional function in the museum, and these can come into conflict. For example, conflict occurs in script development between educators and curators in the realm of exhibition scholarship versus effective communications with audiences. Other conflicts occur in regard to collections protection and exhibition design and object display methods. Loyalty to the standards and best practices of the team member's community of practice presents a barrier to collaboration. For example, a study conducted on this topic revealed a schism between education staff and curatorial scholars who were hired as consultants to an exhibition-planning project. Conflicts occurred over the content of the exhibition in two ways: first, as individuals seeking to win over the team to their content or design solutions, and second, as advocates of their museum functions. Educators were seen as "dumbing down" the messages of the exhibition while reflecting the desire to adopt the latest exhibition design trends. Curators felt that scholarly research should drive the content. Lack of shared knowledge and agreement about best practices in the field exacerbated this situation.[3] These concerns highlight some of the common problems confronting teams. We need to examine how a team can itself become a cohesive and mutually accountable entity.

## Team Formation and Learning Styles

Teams come together under a project charter that lays out expectations, roles, and assumptions regarding the end product. The team begins its work. What now? There are classically four stages of team development.

- forming

- storming

- norming

- performing

These stages reflect the process of creating a high-performing team as described by psychologist Bruce Tuckman in 1965.[4] In the early phase (forming) team members are polite, positive, and even excited about the new project. However, the team will quickly experience work style conflict, stress, and pushback as they struggle with working together (storming). Eventually the team with guidance of the project manager or other facilitator will begin to build trust, acceptable communication systems, and comfort in working together with defined roles and agreed-upon objectives (norming). This then sets up the ability to work collaboratively toward end goals (performing). An example of a process that might work for a museum team is one in which the following activities occur. Begin a dialogue about role expectations, examine the experience and skill of team members, carefully listen to team members, begin to talk about your team as a productive entity among colleagues, build in time for reflection on your decisions, and celebrate milestones achieved.[5] The timing of these four stages is not predictable, although it is important to recognize this progression of team formation. A setback in the team life cycle might occur if a major change occurs in the project, especially the addition of a new member of the team.

### Learning Style Assessments

As every new team moves through the above phases, understanding the impact of individual learning styles will add significantly to the success of the process. There are numerous tools available to determine personality preferences and styles. The value of this is to determine how one operates in a team setting. For example, some individuals prefer to work alone and at a fast pace while others may prefer to research various options before settling on a course of action and completing assignments. These style assessments are not meant to categorize the individual in any negative way. At best they provide insights into the diversity of the team, the expected reactions of individuals in developing projects, and the best modes of communication to assure smooth operations. Unfortunately, not many museum teams take the time to do this assessment during the "forming" stage, if at all. Organizational development specialists have created numerous tools to assess styles. In particular the Myers Briggs Type Indicator developed in the 1960s has been widely implemented in organizations to help managers facilitate successful working relationships. It is here where we learn about introverts, extroverts, decision-making preferences, and ways of reacting to incoming information.[6] This approach is often used in project team development. Other assessment tools that have been developed to support teambuilding include the Four Frames, DiSC, True Colors, and PAEI. Four Frames is a leadership assessment tool developed by Lee Bolman and Terrence Deal described in their landmark publication *Reframing Organizations*. The styles featured here involve the leadership of change in organizations and focus on structural, human resources, political, and symbolic approaches. Theoretically, individuals with inclinations toward any of these preferences will exhibit varied success in leading change.[7] True Colors is an assessment tool popular in organizations since the late 1970s.[8] As outlined in textbox 8.1, the colors match personality traits that line up along the following characteristics.

Findings on these color charts show that these characteristics appear to varying degrees in the population, with orange and gold more prevalent. Your color is not critical, but the personality indicator is. Fortunately, most teams have a variety of these four styles. A similar approach is the DISC system developed in the 1940s.[9] The styles associated with this assessment tool include Dominant, influencing, steady, and compliant. These correlate to task-oriented, people-focused, passive, and outgoing personalities.[10] Any one of these tools might work well for a team considering its internal operations and communications styles. Another popular approach to understanding team differences is the work of Ichak Adizes on learning styles.[11] PAEI was developed in the 1970s as an aid to building a high-performing management team. Theoretically, having each of

## 8.1. True Colors Characteristics

| Blue | Sensitive to Others, Cooperative |
|------|------|
| Gold | Responsible, Organized |
| Orange | Energetic, Risk Taking |
| Green | Intellectual, Visionary |

*Source:* Adapted from Truecolorsintl.com.

the learning styles in the team mix will be most effective for decision making and implementation of projects. The PAEI formula includes four characteristics: producer, administrator, entrepreneur, and integrator. The characteristics of these styles are noted in textbox 8.2.

In completing the PAEI or other assessment tools, team members will often find that they have a mix of all four of these styles, yet one or two will be most dominant. Once these styles are identified and understood, the team can consider communications tactics that will be successful in working among the members. Of course, in the real world it is unlikely that personality traits will drive the selection of team members. However, it can be very helpful for each member of the team to know their own preferences and be aware of the other styles on the team. Ideally all four styles are needed for a high-performing team. We need to have individuals with big ideas and enthusiasm, and those who are able to organize the elements of a project and stay on top of regulations, legal issues, and other accountability requirements. We also want those who are results oriented and will work hard on implementation of good ideas. Finally, we need individuals who will be alert to the culture of the team, the underlying feelings and concerns, and take steps to assure mutual respect and harmony are achieved.

**8.2.  PAEI**

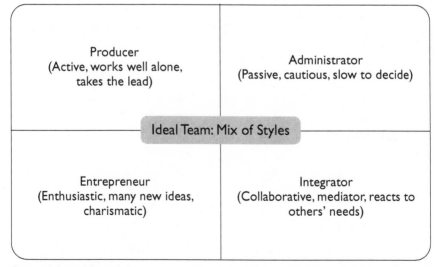

| Producer (Active, works well alone, takes the lead) | Administrator (Passive, cautious, slow to decide) |
| --- | --- |
| Ideal Team: Mix of Styles | |
| Entrepreneur (Enthusiastic, many new ideas, charismatic) | Integrator (Collaborative, mediator, reacts to others' needs) |

*Source:* Adapted from Adizes.com.

## Team Collaboration

Despite understanding individual learning styles, there are other factors that lead to dysfunctional teams in museums. Take the hypothetical example of a project that was conducted without considering team roles and continuity during the life cycle of the project. A mandate to complete a collections inventory involved hiring a group of individuals to survey collections, record their location, and describe them in a new database system. Despite a substantial allocation of funds and several years of work on this project, the results were incomplete and in some cases inadequate to achieving the end goal of a useful inventory system. What went wrong? The project did not receive sufficient priority in the mix of all the activities at the museum, individuals were hired without training in database management systems, knowledgeable curatorial staff failed to consistently support the project by providing needed cataloging data, team members did not feel a part of the larger museum family, project leadership changed several times as did members of the team, and team members lacked mutual accountability. How often does this type of dynamic happen? And what might have been done differently? Despite the problem of integration into the larger extended team of museum stakeholders, this core team was too large and spent little time on developing the all-important levels of trust and respect that are the glue for team success. Patrick Lencioni has written often about effective human resource and leadership systems in organizations. Without the basic trust among team members, no growth can occur. Working collaboratively requires a tolerance of conflict, commitment to decisions, accountability for results, and collective focus on the end results. Various methods of enabling these functions include getting to know team members as individuals, personality assessments, and 360-degree feedback.[12] Teams cannot build trust without time to develop respect. Informal gatherings are a good way to get to know fellow team members as human beings, rather than in their professional role. The end goal is to create a "culture of collaboration" where the team builds trust, masters the ability to compromise, exercises patience, and contributes to a common and sustainable approach to developing projects.[13]

### Communications

This is one of the stickiest factors in team development. Without clear and consistent communications, the team will fail to coalesce and build trust. What are common barriers to effective communications?

- time

- unmanageable personalities

- physical location

- competing priorities

Many teams suffer from the fear of conflict, allow stronger members to dominate conversation, seek to make decisions based on intuition or emotion without using facts, or lack a clear understanding of roles. Without time to devote to communications, decisions can be pushed through without consideration of all factors. Not agreeing on team norms for information sharing, debate, dialogue, and decisions can hamper success. Taking time to explore the various roles and perspectives of each team member can set the stage for later healthy debate. One of the first steps in launching a project is the definition of a shared purpose. Teams need to examine the end goal and agree on what that means in terms of meeting the museum's mission, adhering to its values, and drawing on the strengths of the team members. Is the workload evenly distributed? Are all members contributing to the creative work of idea and design generation? Is there a noticeable lack of ego and "I" statements? Building relationships among the team involves being together in a nonthreatening environment where the focus is on understanding each other. This is where many organizations benefit from offsite retreats, daylong workshops, or informal lunch meetings. The less formal approach allows the team to relax and share common experiences (a great meal, a walk in the woods, a drink in the bar) where fun is a part of the formula for success. Team learning can also involve visiting other museums, reading articles pertinent to the topic of the project, and bringing in guest speakers on related topics to introduce new ideas.

Considering the learning styles models discussed above, there are options for working with team members. The goal is to employ approaches to communications across styles. For example, in the PAEI model, if you are an administrator (cautious and risk averse) working with an entrepreneur (risk taking and action oriented), you have to make some effort to be enthusiastic and positive in presenting your ideas or concerns. Start with the big picture and avoid spending too much time on details. Giving the entrepreneur options to consider may lead to your ideas being understood and accepted. With an integrator, using conversational small talk warms up a discussion that then may need to focus on the best solutions for the overall emotional well-being of the team.[14]

### "Meetings, Bloody Meetings" (John Cleese, 1976)[15]

The most ubiquitous communication mode is team meetings. Whether in conference call, via videoconference, or face to face, meetings are the basic staple of team communications. It is also probably one of the more dysfunctional aspects of teamwork. Meetings can go on forever with little accomplishment. How many times have you attended a meeting and found yourself deconstructing the issues in hallway conversations afterward? Considering our knowledge of learning styles, there are many members of our team who will be daydreaming or multitasking during meetings. Some will be thinking only about what they want to say and not listening to others. In a conversation about a deeply felt issue, it is possible that tempers can erupt and little progress will ensue. One person may feel impelled to hijack the agenda and dominate the conversation. All of these reasons can make the meeting an unproductive experience. How do we correct this? The answer is through planning the agenda and through managing the process. At a minimum, use written meeting agendas with time limits, action items, and follow-up. Before scheduling a meeting, determine if it's necessary. What are the objectives? Is there an urgency involved? Who needs to be there, and what information are they responsible to provide? Scheduling meetings well in advance is important, along with sending out agendas and reading materials and assuring people show up. Meetings should be short. If we are doing an update meeting, perhaps it is a matter of thirty minutes or less. Does it need to be face to face? Meetings that require decisions should allow time for review of the issues and discussion. Items on the agenda should be marked as "information sharing" or "action items." Time limits for each segment also help to keep focus. Set an optimum time limit (not to exceed sixty minutes for example) or build in break time. Once the meeting begins, how do you engage everyone at the outset? Each attendee should have a chance to comment on the agenda before launching in. The meeting manager (project manager or facilitator) should provide ground rules for discussion as well as manage the flow of the meeting. Ground rules can be operating norms, such as:

- speak one at a time

- no whining

- start and stop on time

Facilitating the group process can be like herding cats. Staying on point is important. The facilitator will need to summarize the conversation and acknowledge points of agreement and contention. Often restating the key points made by the attendees can assist with moving forward. A note taker should be present, even possibly writing decisions on a white board or its virtual equivalent if online. Stopping to assure that each group member is feeling comfortable about progress is important. Staying on time is important so that wrapping up an agenda item may require tabling some problem to a later date or assigning a team member to come back with more information. If confusion and disagreements exist, the group should attempt to clarify issues in order to move forward. If not, then the issue should be deliberately set aside for later discussion. This is where a "parking lot" helps. This allows the participants to postpone discussion on a difficult issue. In a meeting that involves a number of people beyond the core team, there may be a need to break into discussion groups (two to four people) to tackle different problems. When people sit silently, they may simply be reluctant to say something stupid. In a smaller group they will no doubt speak up. Recording the meeting's decisions is important. Minutes and action items should be a part of the process and agreed on before adjourning. Using flip charts and post-it notes can be a good way to provide visual record. Today there are varied project management software systems that allow for collaboration online such as Trello, Asana, and Basecamp. These programs link members of a team to a database of activities as well as chat functions. Checking on progress and sharing ideas is easily done. And if workers are at a distance from each other there is great value in this approach.

Meeting facilitators should include everyone in the dialogue via round robins or "check ins" of members regarding how they stand on the issue at hand. Asking each person to share his or her understanding on the issue is critical. As conflicts arise the facilitator should help to safeguard people's ideas. Encouraging people to speak up, summarizing their comments, and shutting down someone who is too negative all fall to the team leader running the meeting.[16] Facilitation of meetings can be especially complicated for the project manager. They must be involved in two major activities associated with group behavior: tasks and maintenance. Focus on tasks includes building the content of the meeting seeking and providing information, summarizing discussions, and testing consensus. Maintenance behavior involves the group dynamics of watching for tensions, encouraging quiet members, and setting meeting norms. As a facilitator, balancing these roles can be challenging.[17] Don't forget the use of humor to keep people relaxed. And refreshments keep the group nourished.

*The difficult person in the meeting.* How do you deal with them? First, you cannot ignore their concerns or their behavior. Acknowledging this is important. Perhaps the person needs to simply be heard. Doing a round robin on the issue may also help. Ask each participant to comment in a positive way. A more mature team will hopefully be respectful of members and be able to speak honestly. If the individual is not willing to work with the team, they may need to be excused from the meeting or even from the project. A one-on-one talk with this disruptive member is also highly recommended. Equally important would be conversations with individuals who go off on their own and do not follow the plan. Crucial conversations allow the project team leader to work with difficult members of the team. Project managers will need to invest significant time in dealing with these problems. The Society for Human Resource Management reports that managers spend as much as 17 percent of their time in dealing with difficult employees.[18]

*Backsliding.* The meeting is over, the decisions are made, actions are assigned, and we are back at work. You are a project team member who needs to implement your assignments. In discussing the action steps with colleagues in your office, there can be any number of setbacks. How to communicate the decisions? What if staff is resistant? Maybe the project team member is not 100 percent sure about their direction. It may be easy to stall on the decision or simply try to renegotiate the agreed-on action, all the while complaining! This may require the project manager's attention to assure that the project does not get off track.

## Making Team Decisions

Aside from understanding the basics of planning and conducting meetings, the project team needs to make many decisions during the life of the project. Agreeing on the goals, the timeline, the budget, the content, and managing inevitable changes require decisions. Sometimes the project manager with consultation from the team will make these decisions. Other times the team needs to work intensely on developing alternatives before a decision can be made. Or sometimes top leadership makes the decision with varying degrees of input from the team. Recall the continuum of participation described in chapter 4. The type of decision depends on urgency, risks, and long-term impact. Team decisions will usually be made via consensus, which is a strength of the team process itself. But consensus may be a poor approach if insufficient data and time are invested in reviewing alternatives. In the early phases of a project or when a significant change is pending, brainstorming is a great way to move a project forward. Here the participants spend time on blue-sky ideas, generating as many as possible to test and further develop. Sufficient time should be invested in considering the options. In a stressful time it might be easy to decide on what the leader of the group or senior manager wants rather than being willing to push back against groupthink. Agile project management systems rely very heavily on this type of decision making. For example, workshops or charrettes are established to bring together teams often with outside experts to develop multiple approaches to the visitor experience. Here it is not unusual to find a room full of makeshift models, post-it notes, and various flipchart drawings. This emphasis on the creative process can be energizing for staff. It might be something that continues into an ongoing program, such as the work done at the Dallas Museum of Art's Creative Connections workspace. Exhibition planner Kathleen McLean has written about the importance of "museum incubators" as "environments to hatch creative new ideas," which often feed the planning for new exhibitions and provide professional development for staff. Museum teams work iteratively, often testing their ideas with members of the public. This approach is extremely important in a world of rapid change, but using these techniques can also clash with traditional planning processes.[19] Sharing your ideas with others in the museum also can be helpful to idea development. Do your post-it notes adorn the hallways, conference rooms, or offices? The National Museum of American History sometimes holds its team meeting in the museum café where any staff member can come by to observe deliberations or add helpful ideas.[20] How do we digest ideas over a period of time?

123

As these ideas begin to take shape, the team can eventually move to idea selection. Project ideas need to be examined for feasibility. as outlined in chapter 5. This will involve a decision system based on context, facts, and input from affected stakeholders.

Communications systems exist beyond the team itself. Any project will ultimately have an impact on the extended team and other stakeholders. Sharing information or even seeking feedback on the project team's ideas and progress is a given. How do we do this in a credible way? Rumor mills within the organization will share stories about the project and its progress and players, so why not be more proactive in doing this? Town meetings to share planning with staff and volunteers, a project website, brown-bag lunch discussions, for key documents, briefing sessions for the board, and meetings with external interest groups such as the press or museum members are all helpful.

## Team Accountability

A critical factor in high-performing teams is the presence of mutual accountability. This can only occur when a team has developed trust and openness in communications. Accountability is simply meeting expectations for delivery of your part in the project. Expectations include timeliness, quality, and working inclusively. It also means agreeing on decisions that move the project forward. Sometimes commitment is difficult. Because team members are busy they may find it difficult to produce their work on deadline. Project managers have a responsibility to work with individuals who are having trouble through one-on-one meetings, individualized training, or negotiating with their supervisors for more time. However, studies show that a high-performing team is not only able to meet deadlines but also exhibits peer-to-peer management. Any team member can quickly raise problems and seek solutions. They don't wait for the project manager to schedule a meeting to discuss a conflict or a problem. Conflict between team members is often resolved quickly and only goes to a higher level if there are major issues at stake. They share stories about their challenges with the rest of the team.[21] This can lead to a rethinking of annual performance appraisals for museum staff. Their team performance is as important as their individual contributions.

## Resolving Conflicts

Conflicts can occur at any point in the team's life cycle. Often the conflict results from unclear roles and authority. Conflicts erupt over decisions about objects, script, funders, space, priorities, and every possible part of the process. Policies and ethical codes hopefully help to temper the issues with guidance. Importantly, a team does not need to stew in these situations. Conflicts can be resolved by listening, negotiating, and compromising, assuring that issues are clear and shared interests are acknowledged. Often, though, the team tries to move on by avoiding confrontation or pretending the problem does not exist. Conflict can be a positive part of team growth. It is a fundamental path to innovation. Managing change is rife with conflicts. In adaptive organizations, the conflict is about ideas, not relationships. The latter can result in avoidance, anger, and inaction—all problems for a team moving forward toward an important end goal. Teams that operate in a status quo mode probably are not going to experience the type of conflict resolution that more innovative groups do. However, in a survey by EMCArts on this topic, 66 percent were not satisfied with innovative approaches, suggesting their lack of skills or direct experience in this regard. Clearly the more experience with this the better.[22] Well-managed conflict will lead to increased critical thinking, less stagnation, and circular thinking, and frequently a renewed energy in the group. The downside of conflict can be a "winner take all" atmosphere, polarization behind different viewpoints, and a breakdown in trust.[23]

### Crucial Conversations

A "crucial conversation" is a discussion between two or more people where: (1) stakes are high, (2) opinions vary, and (3) emotions run strong.[24] This is a well-tested approach to working through and resolving conflicts. Almost always these are one-on-one conversations. They need to occur in a safe environment where respect and trust are present, if possible. Emotions may be high. Listening skills are critical. Dialogue seeks to determine each person's opinions, perceptions, and fears. Participants listen before responding and in doing so restate what they have heard. This acknowledges that the opinions of your colleagues are important. Honesty is important, but so is looking for common ground. What do we both agree on? Are we willing to look for solutions to the situation?

Here a focus on facts, not individual behavior, is absolutely critical. It is so easy to lay blame on someone's actions rather than the situation that confronts you. Recall the importance of empathy in modern leadership theory. When emotions erupt it is time to step back. Stay aware of the need for a safe environment. Silence is okay. Once a path forward is determined, assure that both sides agree in a written document, if possible. National Museum of American History Project Manager Lauren Telchin-Katz, in speaking about conflict, notes, "I work very hard to build individual relationships with my team members. When I need to handle conflict, I do it immediately and either in the presence of the team or individually. I rely on relationships and people skills to resolve the conflict and try to always speak the truth."[25] Telchin-Katz notes that this critical work can take a good deal of time when the stress of teamwork and deadlines are looming.

## Managing from the Middle

Daniel Tuss, an experienced project manager, provides the following observation about the role: "Museums remain egalitarian institutions. With this in mind, effective project management requires more than just the science of managing details big and small, and hinges on the delicate art of consensus building more akin to passing legislation." Daniel has over ten years of experience in the arts at small and large institutions. His work at the Brooklyn Museum as a senior manager provided him the opportunity to manage institutionwide projects focused on acquisitions, internal communications, exhibitions, the ideation of Bloomberg Connect's Ask app, major fund-raising auctions, and programmatic funding partnerships with corporations.[26]

How does the project manager work in this world of conflict, collaboration, and consensus building? In chapter 7 we discussed the dual roles of the project manager as the administrator and the leader. This pivotal role requires a level of neutrality in decision making, with a focus on a fair process. At other times a leadership role will require more vision and inspiration. It is not easy to hop between these. Add to this being ensconced in the middle of the organization where 360-degree communications are the norm. Project managers also have little formal authority and must manage through influence.

The team itself needs guidance at all stages. Project managers meet many challenges in the project life cycle. As a team leader, there is a need for them to model the best behavior. Leading by example can be very powerful. How does that work? Sometimes it is a willingness to be vulnerable with the group. Sharing personal experiences of challenges overcome can encourage the team members to see you as a human being. Leaders are often seen as invincible and the ultimate authority, thus openness is extremely effective in the early stages of building trust. You are a coach, and you must share authority. Each team member will be different and may need varying levels of assistance in doing their job. Some may need additional oversight, or they may need to be listened to more frequently. What determines these differences may be their level of expertise in teamwork or their learning style. Conflict negotiation is also a frequent task with project managers. Clearly one fact we cannot argue with is that building a collaborative team takes time and a lot of patience. What about when team membership changes?

Beyond the team, there is the all-important interface with higher management. How do project managers share information and influence decision makers at different levels of the organization? In larger museums, they may need to work with functional managers of departments as well as the director and board. Higher-level managers are less likely to want a lot of detail, so a one-sheet summary of the project may suffice. If possible, have a meeting of the entire team with senior management. This can build confidence in the work of the team and improve morale of staff involved. Leading up involves a whole set of skills. One thing that is important is to spend some time understanding the way that senior managers like to receive information. They may prefer to learn about your project from someone else. If you have a project director, that individual may be the chief advocate with leadership. Or the advocacy may involve your development director or CFO, depending on what data is at stake. The director may prefer that your project update be made to the entire senior team instead of one on one. Provide information in advance for management to study. Knowing how a senior manager communicates and makes decisions is critical, especially if you need to influence a decision about resources or other major issues. It is important to avoid surprises in communicating up the line.

If a project manager finds that they need to deliver bad news, the first rule is always have options for resolving the problem. Many leaders prefer to have options rather than to make a decision with insufficient information. Allies or expert opinions are also very useful in this situation. You may need to build a coalition among colleagues or other managers to assure that the museum leader is comfortable. If you are in a position to disagree with a top manager, then you may need to ask permission to present an opposing position, and be sure to use facts and not judgments, be humble, show respect, and link your position to the good of the museum. Delivering the message with diplomacy and care is important, but so is being honest with the facts that can lead to success or failure of the project.[27]

## Discussion Questions

1. What learning styles are needed for working on a long-term exhibition development project? Has your museum done this type of personality assessment in regard to team behavior?
2. Consider a situation in your museum that involved conflict among team or staff members. How might the conflict management approaches in this chapter have been used to resolve the problem?
3. Given the need for improvements in management of meetings and internal communications, what solutions work best for a small museum versus a large museum?
4. How do you as a middle manager develop a strategy for influencing senior managers?

## Notes

1. Jennifer Mueller and Julia Minson, "The Cost of Collaboration: Why Joint Decision-Making Exacerbates Rejection of Outside Information," *Knowledge at Wharton*, March 14, 2012, accessed November 12, 2016, at http://knowl edge.wharton.upenn.edu/article/research-roundup-the-dark-side-of-teams-the -risks-of-social-comparisons-and-the-transfer-of-entrepreneurial-skills/.

2. The term applies to a community that extends beyond the museum to encompass a set of best practices in the field. For example, all registrars will adhere to established policies and procedures.

3. Charlotte P. Lee, "Reconsidering Conflict in Exhibition Development Teams," *Museum Management and Curatorship* 22, no. 2 (2007): 183–99.

4. Mindtools, "Understanding the Phases of Team Development," accessed November 12, 2016, at https://www.mindtools.com/pages/article/newLDR_86.htm.

5. Jeanette M. Toohey and Inez S. Wolins, "Beyond the Turf Battles: Creating Effective Curator-Educator Partnerships," *Journal of Museum Education* 18, no. 1 (1993): 4–6.

6. MBTI Basics, The Meyers Briggs Foundation, accessed November 12, 2016, at http://www.myersbriggs.org/my-mbti-personality-type/mbti-basics/.

7. Lee G. Bolman and Terrence E. Deal, *Reframing Organizations* (New York: John Wiley, 2008).

8. Accessed online November 12, 2016, at https://truecolorsintl.com.

9. Accessed online November 12, 2016, at https://www.discinsights.com/whatisdisc#.WCdscldfPdk.

10. In reality, most of the above style assessments lead back to the early theories of Carl Jung, noted psychoanalyst.

11. Accessed November 12, 2016, at https://www.mindtools.com/pages/article/paei-model.htm.

12. Patrick Lencioni, *The Five Dysfunctions of a Team* (San Francisco: Jossey-Bass, 2002), 187–220.

13. Matthew Isble, "Building and Sustaining a Culture of Collaboration," *Exhibitionist* 29, no. 1 (2010): 26–32.

14. See more information on the PAEI model at the Adizes website, http://adizes.com.

15. Anyone familiar with John Cleese's corporate training videos of the 1970s will recall the agony of a poorly planned meeting.

16. Fran Rees, *How to Lead Work Teams* (San Francisco: Jossey-Bass, 2001), 183–94.

17. Thomas A. Kayser, *Mining Group Gold* (El Segundo: Serif Publishing, 1990), 86.

18. Kate Rockwood, "Bad Influence," *PM Network*, October 2016, 48, accessed online November 16, 2016, at http://www.pmnetwork-digital.com/pmnetwork/october_2016?pg=51#pg51.

19. Kathleen McLean, "Learning to Be Nimble: Museum Incubators for Exhibition Practice," *Exhibitionist* 34, no. 1 (2015): 8–13.

20. Personal Interview with Lauren Telchin-Katz, Project Manager, National Museum of American History, Smithsonian Institution, November 16, 2016.

21. Joseph Grenny, "The Best Teams Hold Themselves Accountable," HBR

Blog Network, *Harvard Business Review*, May 30, 2014, accessed November 14, 2016, at https://hbr.org/2014/05/the-best-teams-hold-themselves-accountable.

22. Karina Mangu-Ward, "Survey Results? Conflict Management and the Adaptive Organization," EmcArts, December 12, 2012, accessed November 14, 2016, at http://artsfwd.org/survey-results-conflict-management-and-the-adaptive-organization/.

23. Kayser, *Mining Group Gold*, 146–48.

24. Kerry Patterson, J. Grenny, R. McMillan, and A. Switzler, *Crucial Conversations: Tools for Talking When Stakes Are High* (New York: McGraw-Hill, 2002), 3.

25. Personal interview with Lauren Telchin-Katz, Project Manager, National Museum of American History, Smithsonian Institution, November 16, 2016.

26. Personal interview with Daniel Tuss on February 14, 2017. Tuss currently works as Arts Program Specialist at New York City's Department of Cultural Affairs.

27. Amy Gallo, "How to Disagree with Someone More Powerful Than You," *Harvard Business Review*, March 2016, accessed November 23, 2016, at https://hbr.org/2016/03/how-to-disagree-with-someone-more-powerful-than-you?platform = hootsuite.

# EVALUATING THE PROJECT

P roject evaluation involves a number of activities, including defining metrics, closing down the project, assessing internal efficiency and staff learning, and incorporating lessons learned. Having covered the selection and organization of projects, building the team, and understanding interpersonal dynamics, we know that living through the project is a complex journey. Any number of setbacks will confront a project, including funding, environmental changes, scope creep, and other bumps along the way. Despite a detailed feasibility phase, risk analysis, careful budget development, task analysis and timeline development, and formation of a high-performing team, there are still no guarantees of success! The six phases of a project outline some customary ways of looking at success and failure:

- enthusiasm

- disillusionment

- panic

- search for the guilty

- punishment of the innocent

- praise for the nonparticipants

Although these phases are not completely serious, they highlight that despite all our best efforts there will be mistakes made along the way. People will be unhappy. We need to then take a hard look at the project to determine how to learn from the process and how to measure our outcomes. Metrics of success are always a best practice in the museum field, yet they are hugely illusive and frustrating. Museums do not consistently engage in evaluation of projects although the emphasis on visitor satisfaction and incorporation of stakeholder views is a best practice in the field. However, determining what and how much to measure is still a challenge. How and when do we do this? At a minimum, every strategic plan should include performance measures. Every project will need this as well. In a study by the Project Management Institute in 2016, surveys found that 45 percent of projects are successful and waste less money when the project team and senior management define their end goals, customer needs, and measures of success at the outset.[1]

## Measuring Museum Project Outcomes

What do we measure? Evaluation systems involve setting goals, objectives, and outcomes. The evaluation of a project involves defining performance measures to validate success, justify resources, increase visitation, and stakeholder and staff loyalty. Performance measures include the regular and systematic tracking of inputs, outputs, and outcomes of an activity. The goal is to assess efficiency and effectiveness. We have to choose the right metric for the right goal and weigh the costs and benefits of data gathering. The measurement of inputs and outputs involves project activity. For example, how much money was invested (input) for what products (output)? The latter relate to efficiency measures while outcomes measure effectiveness. Ideally, we want outcome-based measures that provide the basis for establishing accountability for results. This approach is typically what grant-making organizations will expect in funding a project. For example, the Institute of Museum and Library Services has established an Outcome-Based Evaluation standard for a number of years. Grant seekers need to develop a plan that will measure the impact of their project. Did the project make a significant change in serving a social need? For example, the community served by the museum or library has succeeded in educating a certain percentage of its schoolchildren, and this has resulted in an increased number of students understanding their role as environmentally conscious community members. There is the implication of a long-term impact. The output of the program is a school outreach program, a traveling exhibition, or a web-based learning experience; the inputs are the staff skills, collections, or other resources needed.[2]

The concept of performance measurement has its roots in the Total

Quality Management theories developed in the 1950s and widely adopted by for-profits and nonprofits.[3] Although we do not hear this term today, its premises—a focus on the customer, employee engagement, and continuous improvement of processes and products—resonate with much of what museums are concerned with. We design evaluation systems today to include the following:

- to be a systematic approach

- to be based on data collected over time

- to be qualitative and quantitative

- to be focused on results

- to be used to inform decisions about programs, people, and funding

A systematic approach means that we define our end goals and determine our baseline before we measure. Many museums will invest in formative up-front evaluation surveys of visitors or other focus group members. This data is critical in the development of exhibition content. Likewise, a set of summative evaluations will be conducted to assess the outcome of the exhibition once open to the public. Another example is defining the baseline situation before conducting a comprehensive collections database project. Only a small percentage is digitized, and our goal is 100 percent. Our project will include data collected during implementation that will represent progress points. The outcomes will be both qualitative and quantitative. Not only will we see how many objects are digitized but also we will look at the quality of the images, the variety of views, and the associated metadata and how staff and the public use the database. The feedback from these measures will allow the museum to make decisions about new project areas, staff training, and how the project supports core programs such as exhibitions and public access.

Designing an evaluation system requires a thoughtful review of goals and objectives and careful analysis of what data to track. In some museums, performance measures become a burden. Do you really want to know how many staff hours were spent on exhibition design? Do you need to know if the cost per square foot of your building expansion is within industry standards? The answer is not always! Tracking numerous activities can be a time-consuming endeavor, and in the end we may have collected data that no one really cares about. Google analytics allows us to better understand our online activity, but does that translate into the quality measure we really need? When we need to take measures is another factor. It is not always at the end of the project but during its implementation. Nina Simon has addressed this in her book *The Participatory Museum*, stating, "Incremental assessment can help complex projects stay aligned to their ultimate goals while making the project work for everyone involved."[4] And we saw this to be the case with Agile Project Management systems.

What are the measures we use? We can start at the organizational level. A system developed by Harvard Business School in the 1990s is the Balanced Scorecard.[5] Used as a standard framework for evaluation systems in business and nonprofits, the Balanced Scorecard creates a set of performance measures for all strategic goal areas including programs, infrastructure, and resources. Goals for organizations include customer satisfaction, internal business processes, and organizational learning and growth. Ways of knowing that the measures selected are meaningful involves comparison to industry standards or trends. Benchmarking is the collecting of data that can be used for assessing a museum's performance and its relationship to other similar organizations. Benchmarking is done to determine who are the leaders in the field and how well are you doing in comparison. Also in benchmarking there may be activities that can be adopted based on the best practices of other museums.

We can rely to a certain extent on studies, surveys, and other data produced by the AAM, AAMD, and other museum advocacy groups. These are by no means exhaustive, however. Individual data collection and analysis efforts are important sources of information. For example, the University of Chicago's 2010 cultural building survey, *Set in Stone*, analyzed data on new construction in art museums.[6] Another example of comparative research is the study by Anne Bergeron and Beth Tuttle, who cataloged success factors including audience growth, program impact, revenue increases, and the social impact for a number of US museums in their book *Magnetic Museums*.[7]

The traditional way to assess project outcomes is to evaluate numbers. How much money was raised, how many people attended the exhibition, how many positive press reviews do we have, and how many tweets or positive messages appear on Yelp? Numbers often relate to success. Qualitative measures involve the impact of a program on meeting the mission, such as how an educational program improves literacy or reduces obesity or reaches new audiences or provides improved accessibility to disabled audiences. As we have discussed so far, we measure against others (benchmarking), against ourselves (understanding how we change over time), and against industry standards such as the American Alliance of Museums's Accreditation requirements. Our goal is to make a change for the good. What long-term improvements are you making? Since data collection is time-consuming and often difficult to standardize, the museum should think carefully about how meaningful the data is and how easy it is to collect. Many data collection efforts are about inputs and outputs, and few are about outcomes and impact. See textbox 9.1 for a list of customary museum project measures.

## Measuring Internal Operations

In addition to their mission-related evaluation, museums need to look at efficiencies of project operations. How we used our staff time, the funding available, and other resources such as partnerships with outside funders or

---

### 9.1.   Project Success Measures

\* \* \* \* \* \* \* \* \* \* \* \* \* \* \* \* \* \* \* \* \* \* \* \* \* \* \* \* \* \* \* \* \* \* \* \* \* \* \* \* \* \*

**On Time, on Budget**
**Meets Program Requirements**
**Staff Can Operate New Systems**
**Attendance Meets Targets**
**Critical Reaction of Media, Public, & Staff**
**Successful Fund-Raising Campaign**
**Process Worked Well**

---

other museums is important. Fundamental measures we want to always include are:

- Did we complete the project on time and on budget?

- Did we achieve the end goals that were outlined in the project charter?

- If not, what adjustments were made to alter those original goals?

At the end of a project, there are several activities. Have we paid all our bills? Has staff been thanked? Have donors been acknowledged? For exhibitions or building projects, are maintenance systems and ongoing programming for the exhibition handed off to appropriate staff or contractors? Is the exhibition or renovated space useful for public programs or back-of-house operations? Have we done a final report, including accounting? What worked well, and what was a problem? What can we recommend regarding changes in the process or design for the future? Senior Director of Experiences Josh Sarver at COSI in Columbus, Ohio, feels strongly that a process is important for success, but making adjustments may be important. "Having an ideal model for how a project is to be managed at your institution is essential. However, having the ability to mold that process to each project's specific needs is even more important."[8]

Unfortunately, many projects are completed without a formal review process. Staff is too busy with the next project or is anxious to return to their functional office work. Yet the "postmortem" should occur very close to the termination of the project while memories are fresh about the work. It is best to have the project team itself complete this analysis, but often the extended team or other stakeholders will also weigh in. An honest assessment of how the project worked is often painful. If there were cost overruns or frequent team conflicts, it will be hard to face the reasons. Therefore, working with a facilitator or neutral person to conduct such reviews will help identify problem areas and solutions for the future. Individuals on a team may also have some strong feelings as the project terminates. They may have built rewarding relationships with team members and are sad to see those end. The project may have been a high priority and the individual sense of pride in working on it may diminish once it is completed. The team should look carefully at how they interacted and where there were conflicts or communication breakdowns. How well did each member of the team do? In the interest of accountability, the performance of individuals should be evaluated by the project manager based on criteria such as timeliness, enthusiasm, attitude, quality of work, and team dynamics. The team should also evaluate the project manager, the functional managers, and senior staff.[9] Beyond an assessment by the project manager, each team member should reflect on his or her performance. The following questions are helpful in a personal evaluation:

- Were assignments evenly distributed among team members?

- As a team member, did you contribute effectively to the completion of the project?

- Did the team effectively use the best skills of the members?

- Do you think that the team had a sense of mutual accountability?

- What new skills did you learn from this project?

- What additional training would help to improve your performance in future projects?

Codifying lessons of the project and incorporating them into the museum's policies and procedures will add significantly to the project management program. Examples of ways that one can add value from a postmortem would include descriptions of how ideas are generated, the way project management software is used, or strategies for managing contracts. And, of course, celebrate your success! Reward staff for their hard work.

Who gets the final analysis? Aside from the team and senior management, the board should be informed of the success or failure of a project. Policy and procedures may need to be revised to allow for a better outcome in the future. If the project meets all evaluation criteria with high marks, then consider the ways that you can sustain this success. Most importantly, the evaluation phase is one of organizational learning. Leadership should encourage this as part of the museum's culture and operating values. Sharing problems should not be punished but applauded. Worry about blame should not deter the process.

## Incorporating Lessons Learned

The project is complete, the parties are over, and the team has been thanked and is off to other project work. Evaluation data is in hand. How do we use this information? Clearly any outcome or project component that was not successful needs to be rethought for the future. Did the exhibition interactives fail to attract audiences? Were labels too wordy? Was wayfinding a major issue? Did particular design components turn out to be too time-consuming or expensive to produce? Were the team dynamics a problem? Did the museum have too many competing projects to devote sufficient resources to assure positive outcomes? These types of questions that examine both the end product and the process of the project implementation can result in changes that will improve the next project. Sharing results with staff and board will also help the museum sustain itself as a learning organization into the future. This information needs to be a part of any future strategic planning efforts.

An interesting case study involves the work of the New York Public Library. In 2014 they did a large, staffwide strategic planning effort that involved the improvement of services and internal processes. An organization with 2,500 employees, the library began a series of team-based planning efforts to design, test, and implement strategies that would make them more responsive to changing audiences and digitization. The teams were known as "innovation communities" and worked virtually and in person to develop and test ideas over a period of six months. The results of the effort, which involved 10 percent of the staff, led to significant organizational learning and a distinct sense of staff ownership. Chief Library Officer Mary Lee Kennedy noted, "The social bonds created by the innovation communities, we believe, will be integral to the Library's continued efforts to realize its strategic direction." The design and efforts of this planning work reflect the organizing principles of Total Quality Management. Clearly the evaluation of this project was a positive outcome.[10]

## Discussion Questions

1. What types of performance measures are needed in the planning of a collections digitization project? Would these measures be different depending on the type and size of a museum?
2. What are some ways that a project team can analyze their success in a museum project without causing hard feelings?
3. How do you define outcomes for a special event? For an educational school program? Who is responsible for creating outcome statements?

## Notes

1. Field Report, *The Strategic Impact of Projects*, Project Management Institute, March 2016, 6.

2. https://www.imls.gov/grants/outcome-based-evaluations, accessed November 20, 2016.

3. Defined at ASQ website accessed November 28, 2016, at http://asq.org/learn-about-quality/total-quality-management/overview/overview.html.

4. Nina Simon, *The Participatory Museum*, 2010, accessed November 27, 2016, at http://www.participatorymuseum.org/chapter10/.

5. http://balancedscorecard.org/Resources/About-the-Balanced-Scorecard, accessed November 30, 2016.

6. Cultural Policy Center, *Set in Stone*, University of Chicago, 2010, accessed November 25, 2016, at http://culturalpolicy.uchicago.edu/sites/culturalpolicy .uchicago.edu/files/setinstone/index.shtml.

7. Anne Bergeron and Beth Tuttle, *Magnetic: The Art and Science of Engagement* (Washington, DC: American Alliance of Museums), 2013.

8. Josh Sarver, personal interview with the author, November 18, 2016.

9. Sunny and Kim Baker, *On Time/On Budget* (Paramus: Prentice Hall, 1992), 242–48.

10. Bruce A. Strong and Mary Lee Kennedy, "How Employees Shaped Strategy at the New York Public Library," *Harvard Business Review*, December 5, 2016, accessed online at https://hbr.org/2016/12/how-employees-shaped-strategy -at-the-new-york-public-library.

# PROJECT TEAMS IN ACTION

## Case Studies

The varied aspects of planning and implementing projects in museums are best illustrated through the on-the-ground experience of a variety of museums. This chapter will introduce the reader to both routine and innovative approaches to the use of project management systems. The case studies are purposefully a mix of museum types and sizes. The goal is to share how projects actually work in the museum: their relation to strategic plans and mission, the decision process employed to create the project parameters, a description of stakeholders, and the team involved including both internal and external players. Other factors that are featured in these case studies include managing costs, adjusting the project given realities of implementation, team dynamics, and reflection on the lessons learned. Some of the cases involve short-term and inexpensive approaches, while others tell the story of long-term, complex, and high-risk endeavors. In each case the views of the individuals intimately involved are shared. I am grateful to the many museum professionals who provided these case studies and their willingness to share examples of their project's pitfalls and successes. The following topics are covered in this chapter: exhibitions, outreach, new building and renovations, and strategic and program planning. The case studies represent varying sizes and types of museums. These are meant to provide a range of approaches from classic and detailed project management to the streamlined operations of a small to medium-sized museum.

## Exhibitions and Outreach

Exhibitions are the most prevalent type of project in museums, and the case studies in this chapter provide a range of management approaches.

The first case study examines the sophisticated and highly detailed project management systems at a major science museum, COSI in Columbus, Ohio. The case outlines their approach to developing a permanent exhibition. The second case study is that of the changing exhibitions at the National Building Museum in Washington, DC. The Summer Block Party program is an innovative approach to interpretation and visitor experience. The final case is that of a small Canadian cultural center in northern Quebec, the Aanischaaukamikw Cree Cultural Institute. This new museum created an exhibition, *Footprints: Walking through Generations*, for display at their facility and to travel to multiple sites in the Cree community network.

## Energy Explorers at COSI

COSI is a major science center in Columbus, Ohio, and has a strong reputation for innovative exhibitions and science learning programs. The museum has approximately 360,000 square feet and over 150 paid staff, as well as over three hundred volunteers. The museum's mission is to "provide an exciting and informative atmosphere for those of all ages to discover more about our environment, our accomplishments, our heritage, and ourselves. We motivate a desire toward a better understanding of science, industry, health, and history through involvement in exhibits, demonstrations, and a variety of educational activities and experiences. COSI is for the enrichment of the individual and for a more rewarding life on our planet, Earth."[1] In meeting this mission, the museum serves over six hundred thousand onsite visitors annually and an additional four hundred thousand through outreach programs such as COSI on Wheels and Interactive Video Conferencing.

## Project Management at COSI

According to Senior Director of Experiences Josh Sarver, "As an institution we manage countless projects each year varying in scale and scope. These can range from full exhibition builds and traveling exhibitions, to permanent interactives or temporary experiences such as Farm Days, Big Machines, and/or Science Days." Sarver's work group does one or two large-scale projects and three or four medium projects each year. He is responsible for the Office of Project Management at the museum.[2]

The museum's project management process includes a highly sophisticated and detailed set of reviews and documentation to assure accountability. A thirteen-step process is used to develop projects. The first four steps include the definition of ideas, audiences, types of experiences, financial and intellectual resources, links to the museum's strategic plan, and a stakeholder analysis. The latter involves the examination of which individuals both internally and outside the museum will play a role in the project during different phases. This phase is much like the feasibility study process described in chapter 5. At COSI, after the museum's senior leadership team has accepted the idea, the project moves to a preconcept phase involving literature review, front-end evaluation, developing a project narrative and logic model, and an estimated budget and schedule. The museum's development office plays a role at this point, as funding is always a critical factor. The project will not go forward without necessary funding. Assuming that hurdle is met, the museum's project sponsor (a senior-level staff member) will work with the Project Management Office to assign a project manager, develop a statement of work, and create a project organization chart along with a draft schedule and budget. The project is now in development phase, including fleshing out the concept narrative and components, and moves on to a design phase with prototypes and detailed drawings. This leads to the fabrication phase where the exhibition is produced, evaluations are developed, and budgets are finalized, and then to implementation phase, where operations are tested, training on systems occurs, and ongoing maintenance budgets are developed. A final closure phase allows for evaluation of the project based on the logic model, audience responses, and internal operations.

A word about the role of the project sponsor. This individual is not a full-time member of the team but serves as a high-level advocate. Per Sarver, "Due to the problem-solving needs of the role, the Project Sponsor often needs to be able to exert pressure within the organization to overcome resistance to the project. For this reason the Project Sponsor will ideally be a person with great executive and natural authority."

*Energy Explorers* is a permanent exhibition and represents a strategic area of focus for the museum—that of energy and the environment. Exhibition planning began in 2011, and it opened to the public in 2013. In the project charter, the museum assigned staff and determined a high-level budget, timeline, and high-level goals. The following core team roles were included in the charter: project sponsor, project manager, associate project manager, exhibition designer, evaluator, fabricator, and educational program manager. The charter serves as an administrative green light and announcement to the staff that the project is official. An accompanying Statement of Work details the goals and objectives, scope, funding, assumptions, and timeline. The deliverables of *Energy Explorers* included twelve stand-alone exhibition experiences filling 3,800 square feet of space. Notably the project team and project managers were authorized to allocate 50 percent of their time to this effort, acknowledging that they had other work obligations. An interesting component of the project is the stakeholder analysis that outlines the key staff who must sign off on various phases, review or give input to decisions, or participate in one or more phases of the project. This is not always the core project team but other key managers. Acknowledging the importance of these stakeholders and their roles is an important factor in the project management program at COSI. The project was completed in the summer of 2013, a few months later than the original expected opening date.

## Communications and Adjustments

The museum staff uses Microsoft Project software for workload analysis and sharing progress with high-level staff. Individual project teams develop more detailed schedules as needed. Other ways that information is shared is through online systems such as Basecamp and Dropbox. Adjustments to the team over the life of the project at COSI are expected. Sarver noted, "The reality is that we and our stakeholders often take on multiple roles throughout the project. However, it is good to have the ideal model to fall back upon when questions arise regarding authority and expectations." Importantly, the project manager role is usually a part-time assignment, and this is important so that staff gets a number of experiences in working with various functions in the museum. So project managers are assigned more than one project at a time, and should they have any "downtime" they can be assigned to work on another priority project. The museum does rely on outside contractors mainly for construction and fabrication or for specialized work or backfilling when too many projects are running at once. Sarver noted, "If the deadline is fixed, then we will apply more labor to the project or sacrifice some element of the project's performance/scope. Most often though, we use overtime to fill the gap, as we rarely want to compromise on the visitor experience." This is a great example of resource leveling, as discussed in chapter 7.

### Teamwork at COSI

Sarver prefers a small and nimble team. But in reality, the larger cross-institutional model is the one that best serves COSI. This is due to the need for buy-in from staff and support from management. Also mixing skills is essential. In the matter of dealing with team conflicts, the project manager must play a key role. This means "anticipating hurdles before they become an impasse." The importance of coming back to the fundamentals of the project help to keep the team focused. These fundamentals in Sarver's words form an "iron triangle" of performance, budget, and schedule. This need for a disciplined approach cannot be overlooked. When team members are lagging in meeting deadlines in the critical path, delays are a problem.

### Evaluation of the Project

Sarver recommends that involving key staff in the early phase of project development is critical. He uses the following example: "Asking our exhibit technicians (those who service interactives when they are damaged by guests) for their feedback on the design and build of an exhibit will allow the designers and fabricators to make experiences that meet both the needs of the guests as well as the technicians for maintenance; that is, build this exhibit with this certain type of button versus this type of mechanical switch. Once the technicians, designers, and fabricators are on the same page and have empathy for what each work group is attempting to accomplish, they will all have more 'buy-in' to the project's final products. Of course there is some give and take with this work, but as long as the conversation happens early and often in the project, the final product will be much better." Regarding the evaluations for *Energy Explorers*, COSI did a large-scale prototype that allowed them to make changes in advance of the opening. Summative evaluations were done to evaluate both education goals and stakeholder involvement.

Sarver reflects on the use of project management systems by indicating that despite having an ideal model and process, in reality many projects need to be customized. He notes that larger projects benefit from a prescribed process but that small projects do not need this level of rigorous discipline. Sarver has worked at COSI for thirteen years in progressively more responsible positions, all of which support the educational experiences of the museum. As an experienced science educator, he has led various projects at COSI and contributed to many fieldwide outreach efforts. He wisely describes the hard and soft skills necessary in the following statement: "Project management is a balance between science and art. The science is the ability to follow processes and proven procedures. While the art is the ability for an individual to communicate and champion a vision as well as hold individuals accountable to the project priorities, it is these softer skills, the art of project management, where many project managers fall short. Following a prescribed process is straightforward . . . dealing with individual people is where project management gets messy."

The permanent exhibition process is a formal one and involves a highly rigorous process, as we saw in the above description for COSI's *Energy Explorers*. Large organizations also have a greater need to manage diverse resources and stakeholder groups. The next case study features a series of summer blockbuster exhibitions at the National Building Museum in Washington, DC, and illustrates the iterative process of experimenting with new and innovative exhibition themes.

## Summer Block Party at the National Building Museum

The National Building Museum's mission is to "advance the quality of the built environment by educating people about its impact on their lives." The museum has been open to the public since 1985, offering a series of permanent and changing exhibitions and public programs on topics related to the built environment. The museum is privately governed but is housed in a federally owned nineteenth-century historically significant building in downtown Washington, DC. A staff of approximately seventy working with an annual budget of $8 to $9 million manages the museum and its programs. The museum is highly respected in the community as well as nationally. Under the leadership of Chase Rynd, the museum has staged numerous exhibitions and community-focused programs. Notably the museum held a series of exhibitions and other education programs around the theme of environmental sustainability. These efforts received positive public response and support from a variety of funding sources.

In the summer of 2012 the museum embarked on an innovative new program of special exhibitions meant to increase community inclusion and new audiences. The results over five summer seasons (2012–2016) have been extraordinary. The following case study is based on interviews with the project director, Cathy Frankel, vice president for exhibitions and collections.[3] Frankel has been on the staff since 1999 and oversees curatorial, collections, and exhibitions staff. She has prior experience in art museum exhibition management and a degree in museum education. The Summer Block Party exhibitions could be considered "blockbusters" in that they have drawn huge crowds. The exhibitions were created in collaboration with well-known architects, including *Mini-Golf*, designed and built by leading Washington-area architects, landscape architects, and contractors (2012 and 2013); *The BIG Maze* by Bjarke Ingels Group (2014); *The Beach* by Snarkitecture (2015); and *Icebergs* by James Corner Field, a landscape architecture firm best known for their work on New York's Highline. Each exhibition was developed to run a short term, not to exceed three months. The last three exhibitions were staged in the museum's Great Hall, a grand space measuring 316 feet by 116 feet by 159 feet at its highest point.

*Project Management*

The lead functional offices of the museum manage projects, and curatorial staff customarily lead exhibitions. The museum does three to five shows each year. Ideas for exhibitions are brainstormed with curatorial staff and the executive director. For summer programs, the process is more streamlined and experimental in nature. The goal of the Summer Block Party is to create a community space or "town square." With a focus on architectural design and materials of construction, these temporary shows take on the character of an art installation, providing a new view of the great hall space, particularly from the upper balcony of the museum. The experience associated with these installations is a critical component. In developing these ideas, the museum invited architectural firms to work with them. There was no open competition, and they worked with firms with whom they had existing connections. The museum sought ideas that were easy to build (within about three weeks) and low budget. The museum's master carpenter was a key decision maker. Once open these exhibitions placed a lot of responsibility on the visitor services staff that managed attendee flow, ticket sales, and visitor information. The museum hired part-time staff for ticketing and crowd control. The core team included the visitor services office along with Frankel and her staff. The museum's education staff engaged primarily in creating related public programming. Curators contributed to the didactics; development and administrative staff were also involved, but the process is less formal that most exhibitions. Planning for the design involved an iterative approach with the architects finding the most reasonable and economical solution. Implementation occurred in early summer, with about three weeks to construct the exhibition. There are no formal milestone reviews as with longer-term exhibitions. Frankel reports to senior management and the board on a periodic basis. Projects are similar to creating a theater set design and can cost as low as $30,000, with a lot of donated materials and labor. This is an important factor for short-term projects. The museum did a Kickstarter fund-raising program in 2015 for *The Beach*. They also partnered with local restaurants to provide a small food service operation in the space.

*Outcomes*

All of these summer programs have made money for the museum, increased visitation, and diversified their audiences. The summer programs have also been heavily promoted on social media and the mainstream media. Attendance numbers peaked at 183,000 with *The Beach* in 2015. Cutting-edge architects have buzz and draw new crowds. The cost of the projects has increased significantly as the projects have become more ambitious. Despite this, the museum had net earned revenue, and many new visitors who experienced other parts of the museum became members.

*Evaluation*

These exhibitions are reviewed for issues of planning, cost, and staff impact. Each summer program has provided a set of lessons to be applied to the following year. In particular, the museum recognized the need to have more control over the design and to add a visitor services representative to the planning team. Understanding visitor reactions and expectations is a critical factor, especially with a new program. Wear and tear on the museum's carpeting and issues of lighting also were highlights that needed attention after the close of the exhibitions. The museum will also need to set a cap on the cost of these summer programs. The formula has been successful, and the museum is now at a point where they must determine if they want to continue the model on an annual basis. Their strategic plan for 2017 to 2018 included a key action titled "Embrace Innovation" with a goal to develop the summer "block party" into a "museum-wide platform for innovation." Incorporating the summer program into the strategic plan is a good indicator of the museum's new emphasis on capitalizing on partnerships as well as assuring proper evaluation of projects in advance of committing resources.

Unlike the National Building Museum's temporary exhibition program or COSI's large permanent exhibition, *Footprints: A Walk through Generations* represents the work of a new cultural center in a small community in northern Quebec. This project is interesting in that it engages a small and varied team working on an ambitious exhibition that for most is a new experience. Many small, start-up museums will understand some of the challenges that are evident in the ACCI project.

### Special Exhibition at Aanischaaukamikw Cree Cultural Institute

The Aanischaaukamikw Cree Cultural Institute (ACCI) opened to the public in 2011 in the small northern Canadian community of Ouje-Bougoumou, Quebec. Its purpose is to serve as the regional cultural institute for the Cree Nation of Eeyou Istchee, and it includes a museum, library, and archives. Douglas Cardinal, renowned Canadian architect, designed the $15.8 million (Canadian $) facility. The museum building is 18,000 square feet and houses seven hundred objects. They are governed by a board of directors and supported by a community foundation that was instrumental in raising funds for the new building. They have a staff of twelve full-time employees. The mission of ACCI is to be "a living, breathing symbol of the James Bay Crees' determination to preserve and share the stories and legends, the music, the pictures, and the physical objects that show this First Nations people's unique interaction with the land, expressed through hunting, fishing, trapping, and underscored with a reverence for the land they have walked for 7,000 years."[4]

Laura Phillips, coordinator of collections and exhibitions, has been at the ACCI since 2104. Since late 2015, her work there was primarily in support of a new exhibition, *Footprints: A Walk through Generations*, which opened in early 2017. Housed in a 2,000-square-foot space, the exhibition illustrates Cree cultural history and draws on the museum's collection as well as loans from Cree community members. Plans have been developed to travel the show to the ten Cree communities in the Eeyou Istchee region of northern Quebec (land area 5586 km$^2$ / 2,156 sq mi), as well as a special showing at the National Museum of Canadian History in Gatineau in spring 2019. The exhibition is drawn from the objectives of the museum's strategic plan. This particular exhibition deals with "both the dissemination of Cree culture as well as its development and traditions." The exhibition showcases key artifacts and includes educational interactives. The main objective for this exhibit was to develop an experience that could tour the museums in the south of Canada to showcase Cree culture and share a self-curated point of view about Cree life and culture.[5]

## Project Management

The project does not have a formal charter, but Phillips as project manager created a thirteen-page template to outline roles and responsibilities of the core and extended team as well as outline all the key activities and due dates for the project. Phillips shared this with the team and used it as the basis of a quarterly report to the Canadian government granting agency, Heritage Canada. She notes that this template was most important at the outset in setting up the project, especially so for working with contractors and defining team member roles. This project is budgeted at $330,000 Canadian with $200,000 from Heritage Canada. The initial funding was mainly for the on-site exhibition, and further funding will need to be secured for the traveling show and special interactives.

## Project Team

The team is a small group. Staff of the regional cultural center (ACCI) partnered with another community cultural center in Chisasibi.

This partner cultural center was also new, and therefore the two organizations have been learning together. This is the first traveling show produced at ACCI, and all parties were new to this process. The core team consisted of the project manager, one internal curator, a conservator, an external curator, and the five members of the Chisasibi cultural center. The curators and the Chisasibi team were responsible for content research; identification of community artifacts and archival material for exhibition; quality control for exhibition content design; cultural knowledge; and a translation monitor. A contracted design firm played a key role, although they worked from a distance. Despite these challenges, Phillips praised the team for its creative approach to the project.

*Monitoring Projects*

The team met on a regular basis and shared information with the ACCI executive director and other stakeholders. There were a variety of adjustments and changes in the project. Adjustments to the timeline were triggered by vacant positions, vacations, and some lags in communications with the various team members and outside designer. When staff vacancies or vacations occurred during crucial deadlines, the work would often fall to the project manager to complete. Phillips had to undertake critical tasks that were left unassigned, such as to negotiate loans and take care of rights and reproductions. This situation inevitably necessitated revision to the timeline. In retrospect, there could have been more slack time built into the timeline prior to deadlines and milestones to allow for unexpected delays.

The exhibition was set to open in November 2016, but the schedule was revised to open it in January 2017. The team wanted to avoid rushing completion in order to learn fully from the process, which was one of the critical project outcomes. One unforeseen delay not related to staffing was that of text panel production and the need to provide the information in three languages (English, French, and Cree). The proofreading took longer than expected, and they should have had more time allocated in the project plan. Another challenge described by Phillips was developing effective communication with the remote designers (based in Ottawa) using teleconference. The use of subcontractors by the design firm for the graphics work added a new player to the team, and sometimes communications were not as clear. In hindsight, the project team felt they should have anticipated the number of parties involved and their inclusion in the process of design, feedback, and various meetings. It became clear that direct communications with the subcontractors was essential to clarify issues and expectations. When they went through the designer selection process, they did not realize the impact this aspect would have later on during the project when deadlines needed to be met for printing and installation.

Other concerns that faced this team include the reality of customizing the exhibition for travel to a variety of remote community locations. For example, the community of Whapmagoostui is only accessible by aircraft or barge (in summer months only). Difficulty in communications due to the remote location of the cultural center and members of the project team was another challenge. Sometimes their power would go out for days at a time. In other situations they had team members without access to cell phone service or very slow Internet connections, thus Skype was not an option. One unique approach has been to use Facebook to communicate with the community members as well as the content development team about progress on the exhibition. Another unexpected setback is that the lead curator on the staff left the ACCI in October 2016, at a critical time leading up to the installation, thus requiring more input from other Cree staff members at ACCI as well as additional work from the external curator. Despite a number of adjustments and unexpected hurdles described above, Phillips praised her team as both dedicated to the project and a creative group with a lot of excitement and pride. They were extremely skilled at resolving creative challenges, particularly matching material objects and photographs to the themes within the exhibit.

*Evaluation*

As with many similar projects, the ACCI developed an evaluation plan at the time of their grant application in 2014. There are three main goals in the plan, including:

1. A before-and-after analysis of the learning shared among the members of the core team with a focus on the process of exhibition development. As a new organization, that is an important outcome.

2. Enhancement of collections documentation and discovery of important collections materials, including oral histories. Assuring that this information is added to an accessible collections management database according to best practices in the field.

3. Improving and enhancing knowledge of Cree culture and tradition among the members of the community and within Canada as a whole. Both preopening and postopening audience evaluation programs will be included.

In regard to increased audience exposure to Cree culture, Phillips expected good visitorship despite the remoteness of their museum location. There is a strong tourism program in northern Quebec even year round. Marketing efforts will attract audiences from around the country, and there are plans to reformulate the content from the exhibit to create a circulating poster exhibit for the province of Quebec.

Postopening lessons mentioned by Phillips in retrospect include:

1. "Working with a start up 'museum' cultural center—probably true of any partnership: in-depth communication from the beginning, when the partnership terms are being discussed, and for a startup, be thorough in explaining what is expected and get a full understanding in place from all sides.

2. Having a special mandate for a cultural institution makes exhibit content relatively simple because of the limits imposed by the mandate. The challenge for our mandate is that we are a regional center, so we have to be sure to include content that represents all of the Cree communities that we serve equally. The ten communities are united as Cree nations within Eeyou Istchee, but there are many differences, in cultural practice and language dialects, for example.

3. The limited resources from the grant funds meant we had to stick to our agreed parameters and scope throughout the project. Any ideas that could not be accommodated in the budget have been kept for a possible Phase 2 enhancement, which we have applied for separate grant funds for."

Before working at ACCI, Laura Phillips worked at the Wolfsonian Museum in Miami Beach and at Qatar Museums in collections management and documentation systems. Laura specializes in collections information management, museum documentation, and collections management. She is particularly interested in adapting museum practice to support emerging museums and building capacity for museum audiences and museum professionals in new markets. These positions have exposed her to working with different types of collections, a start-up museum, and issues of cultural sensitivity. In considering how a project manager needs to perform given a variety of circumstances and challenges in the museum, Phillips says, "In my experience persistence, creativity, a good sense of humor, being able to simplify complex concepts and explain to non-specialists; a good memory; being able to delegate; being able to match people to tasks effectively; knowing when something is not worth the effort" are the critical abilities of a strong project manager.

Closely aligned with exhibition development are the educational elements of museums. Those can be stand-alone school programs, guided tours, mobile apps, web-based programs, or interactive displays in the museum galleries. The following case study includes the story of the Museum of Flight in Seattle that chose to share elements of its interactive flight simulator program with partner museums around the country.

### Simulator Project at the Museum of Flight

The Museum of Flight in Seattle, Washington, is a major aviation museum with a mission to "acquire, preserve and exhibit historically significant air and space artifacts, which provide a foundation for scholarly research, and lifelong learning programs that inspire an interest in and understanding of science, technology, and the humanities." The museum is staffed by 186 employees and enjoys the services of many volunteers who serve as docents and assist in skilled aircraft restoration, electrical, metal work, and woodwork. The museum serves over five hundred thousand visitors annually and operates on a budget of $16 million. They are the largest nonprofit museum of flight in the world.[6]

The museum does many large and small projects during a typical year. In conversation with me, project manager Rick Hardin noted that he works on three or four major projects and many smaller ones throughout the year. All official projects at the museum are in line with the museum's mission, build goodwill in the community, and some cases are designed to generate revenue. The replication of the Aviation Learning Center (ALC) serves all three goals. The ALC is the museum's highly popular interactive hands-on learning center that contains simulations of the flight experience. The replica project aims to share these exhibits with partner museums. This is a unique opportunity for the expertise of the Museum of Flight to be widely shared with other educational institutions. The museum values its dedication to delivering a quality product within budget limitations. Revenue from the replication project will be invested in other educational projects at the museum. The goal is to create a network of partners that share their experiences in serving their visitors.

The ALC is part of the museum's strategic plan. Hardin notes that the ALC project is in their three-year plan, which "is fairly detailed with a clean scope, detailed estimated budgets and target dates." Despite this detailed planning, "There is still room for innovation and inspiration, if someone comes up with a great idea or an opportunity presents itself and the structure is flexible enough to react."

*Project Management Approach*

The museum does not use a formal charter, but it does use a detailed decision-making process before launching a new effort. The museum uses Smartsheet software for scheduling, cost estimating, and tracking budgets. Excel is often used by individuals and on a more limited basis. Because the ALC project is revenue generating, there is no fund-raising component for its implementation. The project team includes a project manager (Hardin) and several members of the education and technology staff to consult on the goals and work with the partner staff on implementation. The fabrication of the ALC replicas is contracted out. Hardin noted that a "full-sized plane for the 'hangar' part of the program augments the simulators. Having a real plane for the students to climb into is a major asset of the program and key to its success."

The ALC team meets on a monthly basis while the project manager and educator meet weekly. When installation is occurring there are weekly meetings. Hardin keeps senior management informed of progress on a weekly basis and provides bimonthly briefings for senior executives. Adjustments to the project are not uncommon. Hardin has contingency in his budget so that he has some leeway in making adjustments.

*Team Dynamics*

Hardin describes his philosophy for working with the team below.

> I'm a huge fan of communication. I'm very open with what I do and I engage all relevant stakeholders prior to proceeding. If everyone affected is clear on the process I find there is very little conflict. When conflict does arise (it always does), I deal with it again with communication. I try to never dictate a solution. I get everyone together and talk it through until we reach a resolution together. Even if I'm sure of the way things need to proceed, someone else, with their different perspective, may have a better solution. You never know. Doing it together empowers people and lets them take ownership. They understand and feel like they've contributed to the success of the project. In my experience that goes a long way to solidify a team and get everyone on the same page.

In commenting on the role of the project manager, Hardin feels strongly that success in managing projects requires three skills: (1) excellent communications including listening skills; (2) good organization and willingness to be flexible; and (3) taking ownership and accountability for the success or failure of a project.

Rick Hardin joined the Museum of Flight in 2013 in the newly created project manager position, with the challenge of updating the Aviation Learning Center. All of this was in preparation for replicating the enormously successful ALC programs in other institutions. Hardin also manages other large projects with facilities, education, and the exhibits department. Hardin brings to the museum more than twenty-five years of trade show and museum exhibit construction project experience.[7]

## Museum Building Projects

Museums frequently are engaged in construction projects, some of which can last for many years. The following case studies provide the view of one large and one small museum building project. They reveal many similarities in project impetus, grounding in strategic plans, staff involvement, community response, and outcomes. The size, cost, and time commitments are vastly different. In addition, there is a noted difference in regard to the project manager. The larger project at the Denver Museum of Nature & Science selected a trusted internal staff member to serve as project manager along with the facilities director as "team captain." The smaller project at the Bennington Museum used the services of the design/build company as project manager working closely with the museum's director. The selection of an external consultant to manage a project is a good idea when the client does not have extensive experience or has many other priority projects. Outside firms can help in selecting the best contractors, creating the initial budgets, and importantly, advising the museum on options as they proceed on key activities of the building projects. And this was certainly the case in both of the projects illustrated in this chapter.

## Denver Museum of Nature & Science Education and Collections Facility

The Denver Museum of Nature and Science (DMNS) opened its new wing, the Education and Collections facility, in 2014 after six years of active planning, design, and construction. The museum has undergone a number of expansions since it opened in 1908. The genesis of the new 126,000 square foot, $56.6 million facility was in a new strategic plan created under the leadership of president and CEO George Sparks. The expansion project is considered exemplary for its design and planning approach, having achieved goals of creating a modern collections preservation facility and a space to host education programs and changing exhibitions. The new wing received a number of awards, including the Midatlantic Association of Museums's 2017 national Buildy award. This case study features the project management aspects of this expansion and is based on interviews of key project staff, including Peggy Day, Project Manager; Elaine Harkins, Facility Director (ret.); and Kelly Tomajko, Director of Collections Operations. Importantly, the project was completed on time and practically on budget (just $6,000 over estimate). This is unusual for a major building project.[8]

*Motivation*

At the time of the museum's 2005 strategic plan, there were forty-nine separate spaces throughout the facility used for collections storage. This is a major museum (in 2016 the museum was staffed by four hundred individuals and supported by 1,800 volunteers, working with an operating budget close to $40 million), with many competing needs and interests. Fortunately, the new strategic plan emphasized the importance of collections stewardship and responding to science education standards. The museum staff began their work with benchmarking other similar museum projects. The resultant planning for both a collections facility and an education center led to the application for a bond proposal to the city and county. The proposal was accepted by the city council, and subsequently voters approved a $70 million cultural construction bond issue in November 2007, $30 million of which went to the museum for this project. The City of Denver has over the years invested significant resources in their cultural facilities, illustrating a strong community connection.

*Planning*

In 2008 a core team of staff created a project charter and project development process that was then approved by the museum's senior leadership team and board of trustees. The charter included a description of the project, the goals, a statement of need including the recognition of STEM challenges in the schools, visitor amenities, technology infrastructure, along with collections preservation and access. The charter also identified anticipated external audiences and internal users, a broad timeline, assumptions about energy savings goals, and collections space and education center needs. It further defined funding requirements, issues for consideration, core team composition, operating guidelines, and a preliminary timeline. These elements are comprehensive and include the broad spectrum of factors typical for this size of project. The charter also included a set of operational guidelines, including a commitment to using project management principles such as approved milestones, and a small core team with responsibility for delivery on time and on budget.

*Project Team*

The core team included individuals representing education, exhibits, collections, sustainability, technology, and facilities, as well as a senior leadership team "champion" and a project manager. This composition allowed for the interests of all the key stakeholders, specialists, and senior-level staff to be represented. This team worked closely together for six years. Despite changes in team membership (turnover in the education and technology departments), the project proceeded on schedule. Fortunately, one important factor in staying on schedule was the funding available to backfill key team members so that they could devote full time to this priority project. The team was also augmented by a number of external consultants providing critical services to the project. These included architecture, engineering, cost estimating, space planning, construction, LEED certification, security, exhibition design, and internal systems commissioning.

## Timeline

The phases of this project included strategy, feasibility, concept development, design, construction documents, permitting, actual construction, and postinstallation. A Project Development Process document was created in Microsoft Excel and updated as needed throughout the project. This document included the responsible team members, decision points and milestones, senior-level review, and other checkpoints. Teams did break into subgroups such as facility, sustainability, operations, technology, and fund-raising functions. Their early planning phase lasted approximately two years. The museum broke ground in 2011 and opened the new wing to the public in February 2014.

## Financing

The project included the $30 million bond issued by the city as well as funds raised from foundations, government agencies, individuals, and corporations. As a result of these generous contributions, the museum was able to secure the $56 million necessary for completing the building before it opened to the public. In addition to the $56.5 million for the building, the museum received federal grants from the Institute of Museum and Library Services, National Endowment for the Humanities, and National Science Foundation to help fund the collections storage systems. In addition, two foundations made significant gifts to the project. The Avenir Foundation contributed funds to name the Avenir Collections

Center and the Avenir Conservation Center and to endow a conservator position, while the Morgridge Family Foundation provided funding for a family learning center. Project staff noted, "Because of this conservative financial approach, the Museum has not experienced any financial setbacks related to the project, and in fact completed the project without incurring debt."

The building as finished serves both education and preservation and collections access functions. Five levels include three dedicated to education and special exhibitions and two dedicated to collections, including conservation, processing, office space, and room for volunteers, object study, and storage. A discovery zone, science learning studios, and flexible temporary exhibition spaces greatly improved the museum's ability to provide quality educational programming. Visitation since opening has been on the rise, topping 1.7 million in 2016.

From the perspective of the staff and the public, the finished facility has been a big success. The internal museum stakeholders, particularly the research and collections staff, are thrilled. Levels of security, cleanliness, air quality, safeguards to mitigate water intrusion, and state-of-the-art storage furnishings were the result of careful planning. One of the consistent messages shared by the team members I interviewed was that they were trusted to make the right decisions for the new facility. Having this level of decision authority led to pride in the final product and confidence in the quality of the design.

*Project Team Highlights*

The team members interviewed all spoke to the value of a small and nimble team, the importance of a project manager with experience in museum operations and strong internal credibility, functional advocates on the team, and an owner's representative (Harkins, museum facilities director) who could interface with the external consultants and contractors. They also underscored that management relied on them as a decision-making body on operations and budget given authority to prioritize design decisions. As a result, the team members saw this project as a model for the field. They did, however, acknowledge some delays, such as scheduling the manufacture of storage cabinets once punch-list items were addressed and raising additional funds for endowment.

Some specific feedback from core team members provides insight into the complexity of managing such a large project with many players and a lot of community expectations. In particular, seasoned staff members worked on this project, bringing years of experience to the project. The project team "captain" Elaine Harkins completed many facilities projects in her twenty-seven years at DMNS. Her experience matches that of Project Manager Peggy Day, who has had thirty-one years at the museum. These two individuals handled the internal and external communications. Harkins (who has recently retired from the museum) hired a capital projects manager to assist with other bond-funded capital projects. The capital projects manager also coordinated with the city during installation of the building infrastructure to attach to existing city systems. As the owner's representative, Harkins was responsible for coordinating between design and construction functions. This also importantly included interface with the external contractors and consultants in both the design and construction phases. She represented the voice of the museum during the design and construction of this new addition project, coordinating the needs of the education, programs, exhibits, and collections user groups with the overall goals for energy efficiency and sustainable design elements.

*Communications*

The team met every week during the design phase. A Construction Manager General Contractor (CMGC) was hired at the end of schematic design to be there during the final design, and this assisted greatly in creating realistic cost estimates. A setback came when the original design architect's availability was curtailed just as key decisions were needed. This might have been avoided in the original contract. Harkins was successful in her role, as she understood how to read contract documents as well as construction drawings to assure that the contractors remained accountable. The project did get behind by six months, but despite this it opened on time. So in the end there was less time for making adjustments in a break-in period for the new spaces.

A lesson learned from Harkins's perspective is to be prepared as "change always happens," and in the case of this project there was a change in personnel in the education and technology departments that did impact some design decisions. As Harkins noted, there is value in everyone understanding the full project so that a loss of a key player will not disrupt planning or implementation. Another lesson was that a specialist in LEED design was needed to assure compliance with requirements for certification. The postopening commissioning and other issues that are typical of this large a project included continuing adjustments to the humidity levels in the collections area.

Kelly Tomajko, with nineteen years in the Research and Collections Division, was a key member of the core team as the advocate for the collections. Her role was to assure that decisions were made to accommodate collections storage, conservation, staff, and volunteers. Concentrating functions in a new wing was a dream come true for the long-term preservation goals of the museum. Exercises in collection planning, collection risk assessment, and collection space analysis were launched in 2004. Generating plans and data well in advance of the fast-paced design and construction process was key to the success of the Avenir Collections Center. Some highlights include the aggressive mitigation for water intrusion, creating separation between building systems and collections, between clean and dirty activities, and between work and storage spaces; creating concentric zones of cleanliness and security; and inclusion of equipment for health and safety such as fume hoods and emergency showers. Tomajko benefited from a backup team in her department so that she could invest the needed time in working on the expansion. Her work on the core team was a great opportunity to have input into operational decisions as well as budget priorities. She also worked on testing ideas through sharing decision options with her backup team. This is a great example of leading from the middle, where staff has the ability to collaborate on critical decisions. In hindsight, Tomajko notes they got everything they wanted. A testimonial to a successful project! She managed a separate $10 million budget for FF&E (furnishings, fixtures, and equipment), collection storage, and moving collections into the new facility. She is now responsible for the operational success of this state-of-the-art collection facility for its various user groups, and works to align collection preservation practices with institutional and environmental sustainability.

*Project Manager's View*

The DMNS uses project management approaches in major initiatives such as exhibitions and facilities. The expansion project manager Peggy

Day has had considerable experience in the museum working in marketing that gave her good cross-functional organizational skills. This was likely the reason the senior management selected her to serve as project manager. Day has been with the Denver Museum of Nature & Science for over thirty-one years and is currently the director of strategic projects. She has had many duties with the museum, including product development, marketing, community relations, funding and bond elections, and the new Education and Collections Facility. In her project management role on the expansion, she led the internal team from planning through move-in and managed RFP's, contracts, schedules, budgets, approvals, city compliance, and internal communications. Her duties also included setting up the internal core team and project timeline, handling compliance with the City of Denver on the $30 million bond funding, and meeting regularly with the team, architects, and contractors. As the museum moved to the construction phase, her work shifted to monitoring the project by working with the team. Day mentioned the change in key personnel on the team, including education and technology staff, and that adjustments to the timeline and implementation schedule were a result. As discussed in chapter 6, their need for "resource leveling" included hiring consultants to assist with technology portions of the new facility. Adjustments to the budget were a reality, and decisions often meant that "value engineering" or modifications to the scope or types of systems or materials was needed to assure that the museum adhered to their budget goal.

Communications and project monitoring were a key component of Day's job. She did not use any complex software to monitor the project and update data. This is largely because sharing information with the team and other stakeholders requires a "simple system." She indicated that it is "important to show it and understand it." For museums this is almost always the best solution. For sharing information with the larger staff there were all-staff meeting updates, and frequent reports were made to the senior leadership team, the trustees, and the city.

The project did open on time, although as mentioned earlier there were some delays in getting into the facility in advance to test out the technology, security, and other systems.

*Evaluation of Success*

Peggy Day noted that the museum did preliminary work on a comprehensive and formal postmortem evaluation at the end of the project.

As with most projects, the staff was immediately engaged in ongoing operations and other projects. Day states, "While no formal evaluation for staff and public have been implemented, there has been constant tweaking to make sure systems and processes are working efficiently." Their experience certainly mirrors that of many museums interviewed for this book.

Not all museum construction projects are as detailed and time-consuming as the Denver case study above, although it is clear that any facilities project will be a major draw on the time of staff and board members and impact membership and community. All types of museums experience renovation, new building, or major retrofitting of infrastructure to meet their mission, protect collections, and serve the public. The following case study was written by the Bennington Museum's former director, Steven Miller, and describes his experience of working on a needed renovation and expansion to improve facilities management and museum programs.

## Renovation and Expansion Project at the Bennington Museum

The Bennington Museum is a regional history and art museum located in Bennington, Vermont. The town of about sixteen thousand is in the far southwest corner of the state, and thus the museum includes parts of nearby New York and Massachusetts in its history and contemporary art overview. Tracing its roots to 1852 as the Bennington Historical Society, the museum established its current location when it took over an abandoned stone church in the 1920s. In time it evolved into a larger complex when additions were made to accommodate its growing collection and exhibition needs. By the end of the twentieth century a more robust exhibition schedule was unfolding, storage was full, public programming space was inadequate, and infrastructure improvements were essential. Architectural changes had to be made if the museum was to meet new challenges and not stall, or worse, regress.

When I (Miller) was hired as executive director in 1995, it was critical to reconsider the museum's operations and public programming. Fortunately, very positive core mission elements could be built upon as they had long been appreciated and embraced locally and by tourists who especially enjoy Vermont in the fall. No changes in the reason for the museum's existence were necessary. The collections were superb, and while adjustments were necessary in a few areas, there was no reason to avoid a continued emphasis on excellence in content maintenance and acquisitions. The area of difficulty fell into how the museum offered its variety of programs, activities, and events. These were popular but often shoehorned into spaces that were never designed for such use. There was not enough room to accommodate the participation levels that were clearly possible.

To prepare for improvements, I drafted a strategic plan. It was based on observations made as visitors engaged with the museum, from their arrival to their departure. Pertinent staff involved in my overview recommendations included the building manager, collection manager, and the manager of the admission desk and sales shop. This was submitted and unilaterally approved by the board of trustees with no changes. In addressing the physical plant, the plan called for renovations and expansion options to: (1) provide dedicated public programming space; (2) improve gallery use and visitor circulation; (3) increase and improve collection storage; (4) correct peculiar architectural anomalies, such as expanding the sales shop and connecting the Grandma Moses Schoolhouse to the museum so it could be used in the winter; (5) upgrade infrastructure such as HVAC; (6) make the whole museum accessible for people with disabilities.

The emphasis on public program space was especially important in consideration of a bypass highway that was to be built around Bennington. I estimated this would reduce what I called "drive-by drop-ins" by 30 percent. This is exactly what happened after the bypass was completed and traffic in town ebbed substantially. Fortunately that loss of visitation was made up for with other audiences. These included special interest collectors in the area of American pottery, quilts, and furniture. The museum has the best collection of nineteenth-century Bennington pottery, made in the town. The quilt collection is small but holds one of the nation's most famous historic quilts. The Jane Stickle Quilt was done by a group of women during the Civil War, and their names and a personal note are on each piece they sewed into it. The furniture collection is heralded as one of the finest regional holdings of its kind in any museum.

## The Project

The renovations covered about six thousand square feet. The expansion covered about fifteen thousand square feet. The total cost was $2.2

million. (An additional $400,000 was raised to enhance the endowment.) The design process went fairly quickly. It was completed by the design-build firm and approved by the board of trustees in about four months. Permitting was easy as the area is rural, and few town or local building requirements needed to be followed. Any state regulations and environmental laws were met with no difficulty by the contractor. This was a nonunion job, but the museum was interested in meeting prevailing wages. It took about three-quarters of a year to complete construction.

Existing (as opposed to new) museums generally have two options when engaging in major construction projects: close for the duration of the work or stay open. There are pros and cons to both, and neither is preferable as there are adverse repercussions to both. Closing can have a negative impact for staff who are laid off. It also halts public attendance practices, and regaining lost visitors can take some time after a project is finished. Staying open is tough on staff who have to do their jobs in and around the inconveniences of an active construction site. The Bennington Museum remained open during its construction project.

*Stakeholders*

There were no specific stakeholders other than the community the Bennington Museum served and a few major financial donors to the project. That community consisted of various audiences including local residents, residents of Vermont generally and nearby parts of New York and Massachusetts, tourists, and collectors with specific subject interests such as early American furniture, American ceramics, regional American art, and quilts. For the duration of the project, a key stakeholder group I designated consisted of local contractors, be they for plumbing, electrical, HVAC, architecture, construction, and others. The Breadloaf Corporation (the company who designed and built the project) was instructed to solicit bids from companies in the area, provided they qualified for a particular task. The firms had been in business a long time, and in many cases the employees were literally museum neighbors. Some companies were already familiar with the museum, having done work for it in the past. An example was a roofing business familiar with slate roofs. With proper vetting for the expansion and renovation, it was awarded the roofing contract. This practice was sustained throughout the project and is one I recommend, especially for museums in small communities where local public relations is critical to success.

Other stakeholders were financial donors who supported the project in various significant ways. Private "hard hat" construction tours were arranged for them. Midway through the project work was halted so a wonderfully formal lunch could be hosted in the middle of the site. The dichotomy between elegantly set tables and a specially catered meal was fun when surrounded by ladders and scaffolding, piles of lumber, electrical detritus, tool chests, and ground cloths. In addition to private tours, regular media alerts were issued to provide updates.

## Project Team Members

A member of the Bennington Museum's Board of Trustees was the trustee liaison. This proved enormously helpful as sometimes trustees listen to each other more than they do staff. Though I had devised the renovation and expansion plan and was the museum point person throughout the project, I worked very closely and quite productively with the trustee liaison. The architect was the point person for the Breadloaf Corporation and served as project manager. Several staff was essential to the success of the project. These included the building manager and the collection manager. The former was the person who worked most closely with the contractors as he knew the inner workings of the museum far better than anyone else. The collection manager safeguarded the collections during the project.

## Frequency of Meetings

Meetings were held weekly between the museum and the design-build firm. Information was shared at these meetings, and more often when necessary. The museum did not use any specific software for its record keeping or other communications. Minutes were recorded for all meetings and approved by all participants. The Breadloaf Corporation and the museum kept these on file.

## Financing the Project

The project cost $2.2 million, and the board of trustees and the museum director raised $2.6 million privately. The campaign was treated as a public fund-raising venture. Trustees and the director, approaching potential major donors, made appeals one on one. Several individuals made important contributions, and a few prominent "naming" opportunities were put in place. The museum had not done such a campaign in many decades, but the board of trustees was more than willing to engage in the prospect cultivation process and ask for support. Initially a consultant was hired to advise on the campaign, but his services were quickly dispensed with as the trustees embraced their responsibilities to seek and get funding. Museum expenditures, which were largely scheduled payments to the design-build firm, were handled by the museum's bookkeeper under the oversight of the trustee liaison, the treasurer of the board of trustees, and me.

## Outcomes and Evaluation of Success

The project has been enormously successful and meets all desired outcomes. The public program spaces are in constant use and serve the purpose to expand community involvement. The communities vary and include local residents, those with special art and history interests, and tourists. The handicap-access improvements have had an obvious beneficial impact. Structurally the project seems to have no drawbacks, and no major changes or corrections have been necessary.

## Lessons Learned

1. Substantial museum construction and renovation projects are extremely complicated. Few people understand the magnitude or nature of the details, nuances, ramifications, scheduling, or disparate pieces that must fit together to make it all work. Unless they have some experience in such matters, museum trustees and staff must be especially mindful when it comes to planning and running projects in a knowledgeable manner. From the actual construction perspective, the key person of utmost importance for a project is the project manager. He or she is the point person between the client and everyone who does actual work on the job site.

2. Unless they have experience designing museums, most architects have no idea how museums work. They must be schooled in what component architectural spaces are needed, why, and how they interrelate. It is

imperative that knowledgeable and appropriate staff set the initial program and constantly follow through on its implementation. Architects can be cooperative in this respect or not. Beware of architectural "teams" for a project. All too often this obfuscates any one person being responsible for any one aspect of a project. Circular ignorance can be the constant norm. I recommend that the same single architect be always available and always responsive in a timely manner throughout a project. This arrangement can be understood and agreed to when a construction project proposal is announced. And it must be adhered to rigorously.

3. Every museum that was purpose-built was ideal the day it opened and served all the functions anticipated. The next day it didn't. This is an exaggerated way of explaining that different museum folks have different requirements of "their" museum. When additions were made to the Bennington Museum in the past, they did the job they were designed to do. Over the years, as a result of upgrades in museum profession standards and greatly expanded public uses for these institutions, past improvements proved inadequate. As museum staff and trustees come and go, and expectations and requirements for museums change, space needs change. What might have been sufficient initially at times proves insufficient. For example, in 1900 less was required of museums when it came to food service and retail sales. Space to provide these services was limited, if present at all. Today eating facilities and sales shops have a high priority that in turn is reflected in architectural planning.

4. It is important to note that "change orders" issued during a project are to be expected, especially when substantial renovations are happening. Such changes do not in and of themselves suggest a building project failed or had significant drawbacks. Stuff happens. With the exception of one aspect of the project, the Bennington Museum work was accomplished in an exemplary manner. When winter arrived the first year after the project was finished, it was discovered that the Grandma Moses Schoolhouse was not insulated. This fact had been completely missed by museum staff, the architect, and construction folks. Because the Schoolhouse was now connected to the main museum building complex, when the first winter rolled around arctic air came breezing into adjacent galleries. Needless to say, this oversight was quickly corrected!

Steven Miller has been in the museum profession for forty-five years. During his career he has served variously as a curator, director, and trustee with leading history museums in the Northeast. He served as director of the Bennington Museum from 1995 to 2001. He is currently the executive director of Boscobel Restoration, Inc., Garrison, New York. He has written, lectured extensively, and taught classes on a variety of museum issues.

## Small Museum Project Management Systems

The vast majority of museums in our country are small museums. That does not in any way prohibit the use of project management techniques. Experienced museum leaders and boards are well aware of the importance of strong management programs and assuring that staff are given opportunities for training as well as the leadership aspects of working on projects. The following case studies are not meant to chronicle specific projects, but the ways in which small organizations apply best practices. The Abbe Museum in Bar Harbor, Maine, has used project management systems for several years and developed a suite of templates for their projects. The Shiloh Museum of Ozark History in Springdale, Arkansas, also has used project management for a vast array of their core programs. Finally, the Michigan Museums Association, although not a small museum, is actively employing project management at all levels of operation in an innovative, yet highly practical, approach. Many of their members are from smaller museums.

### Abbe Museum

With the mission to "inspire new learning about the Wabanaki Nations with every visit," the Abbe Museum offers changing exhibitions and a robust programming schedule for all ages, welcoming thirty thousand visitors each year. Wabanaki people are actively engaged in all aspects of the museum, from curatorial roles to policy making. The museum operates two facilities: in Acadia National Park and the other in a renovated historic landmark building in downtown Bar Harbor, Maine. The museum is a Smithsonian Affiliate, an active member of the International Coalition for the Sites of Conscience, and an involved community anchor. They hire over thirty Native artists and demonstrators to lead programs for schools and public audiences, serve on advisory committees and as content specialists, and represent over eighty Native artists in their museum shop. As a decolonized museum, the Abbe shares authority with Native communities regarding documentation and interpretation. The museum has a staff of seven and annual operating budget of $1,000,000.[9]

Project management at the Abbe is applied mainly to exhibitions and events, although they are implementing it more widely with a new strategic plan. The role of project manager falls to the functional office head, such as exhibitions being managed by the manager of creative services. The president and CEO, Cinnamon Catlin-Legutko, holds the role of project sponsor. The museum uses templates to organize the work of project teams such as the Exhibit Plan Template. This is not a formal project charter but is used to kick off projects and establish timelines, budgets, and milestones (see Appendix A). Project teams are led by experienced individuals with the "ability to organize and communicate." One point made by Catlin-Legutko is that "communication is our weakest area for our teams. Since we are so small, we typically lock and load and get moving, but forget to keep each other apprised of decisions and developments." The museum creates project timelines in a table format using Excel or Asana. Budgets are developed by the project manager, approved by the CEO, and integrated with annual operating plans that are approved by the board.

The Abbe also takes care in meetings to set agendas, create notes, adhere to time frames, and be sure that the right people are at the table. As with other museums I interviewed, the Abbe staff takes advantage of sharing their meeting notes on Google Docs. The online system Asana is also used to update projects. Project adjustments occur in regard to staff assignments based on the skills needed, particularly with a transition to a new team member. In regard to budgets, the museum relies heavily on funds raised, and thus "if we haven't raised enough money by a certain time, project timelines are altered."

Of particular concern to the Abbe is effective team dynamics. Catlin-Legutko notes, "We've studied Patrick Lencioni's work for years and believe in productive conflict. So, essentially we anticipate moments of conflict and discuss them before they become an issue. Managerially, though, we make sure we have regular check-in meetings with our direct reports and make sure there is ample air to discuss issues and concerns.

However, if things start to boil over, we make sure to meet privately and break down the issues."[10] The Abbe prides itself in being an inclusive organization. Additionally, staff is encouraged to take courses in project management and leadership skills that are critical to the success of their projects. In regard to the evaluation of the team process, the Abbe has a postmortem template that is used for exhibitions and events. In every case the team will work to create a lessons-learned evaluation for future projects.

One unique aspect of their project management program is the development of a committee charter for board operations. This charter is a detailed outline of the issues and concerns or board committees that Catlin-Legutko feels is important, especially for a small museum where board and staff work closely on day-to-day issues. (See the Appendix for examples of the Abbe's exhibit plan template and postmortem evaluation along with the board committee charter.)

Working in museums for more than twenty years, Cinnamon Catlin-Legutko has been a museum director since 2001. Prior to joining the Abbe Museum as President/CEO in 2009, Cinnamon was the director of the General Lew Wallace Study & Museum in Crawfordsville, Indiana. Her museum service includes board membership with the Maine Humanities Council and AAM. She is an expert on small museums, having edited the Small Museum Toolkit in 2012 and revisions to *Museum Administration 2.0* in 2017.

## Shiloh Museum of Ozark History

The Shiloh Museum of Ozark History was established in 1968 as a municipally funded museum interpreting the history of the Arkansas Ozarks and is located in northwest Arkansas, one of the fastest-growing and economically thriving metropolitan areas of the country. Their mission is to "serve the public by preserving and providing resources for finding meaning, enjoyment, and inspiration in the exploration of the Arkansas Ozarks." As a municipal museum, the City of Springdale, Arkansas, governs the museum, with authority for policy and budgeting vested in the museum's board of trustees. The museum has a staff of eleven full-time and one part-time employee. Situated on a three-acre wooded site, the museum is composed of a 1991 museum building and seven historic structures reflective of the early Shiloh community. The museum cares for over one-half-million artifacts, a million images, and other archival holdings. Their operating budget is just over $750,000.[11]

*Museum Planning and Project Management*

The museum's director, Allyn Lord, considers many of their activities as formal projects, such as those that include a staff/board collaboration and that require detailed schedules and budget oversight. Lord notes, "Museum projects could include activities involving facilities, exhibitions, programs, collections, events, research, technology, fundraising, strategic planning, and/or marketing." Like most museums, strategic planning drives Shiloh's projects. Per Lord, "Strategic plans specify the team which is assigned, oversight of each goal/action step, and can include staff members, board members, committees, volunteers, and occasionally community partners." Projects also include facility improvements, programs associated with key anniversaries, or individual departmental goals. Lord explains that "annual programs, exhibits, and events are discussed and scheduled each February for one or more subsequent years, and projects can arise from those discussions. Staff members and teams are most often at the helm of these projects, with supervision from the director."

*Launching the Project and Forming the Team*

The process to initiate a project involves an introductory meeting with all participants. From this results a project plan including a Gantt chart and team assignments. As a small museum, the Shiloh project teams are often composed of staff, board, and community members and volunteers. An example would be the *Ozark Journey: Instrument Makers of the Ozarks*, a grant-funded project that involved a traveling "mini-museum" with music, artifacts, storytelling, and school curriculum that served elementary schools. The emphasis of the project was to highlight outreach to small towns and underserved communities in the region. The museum team included their outreach coordinator, education specialist, folk duo members, the director, and representatives of the University of Arkansas and a local middle school teacher. The outreach coordinator led the team. As noted by Lord, "A team usually involves a project director (who may or may not be the team member who oversees budget), staff and/or board members with project-related expertise, folks outside the museum who are volunteers or contracted employees, and member(s) who deal with evaluation and (if applicable) report writing."

## Project Manager Role

At Shiloh, project directors, who take responsibility for managing team efforts, lead projects. Most staff will have the opportunity to step up to this role. As Lord notes: "That person may be the museum director, a staff member, or a board member, depending upon the project. Grant projects will have a predetermined leader, as will strategic-plan-related projects. Departmental projects are almost always led by the department staff member." When contractors are involved with a project, the project director and/or the team member with the related expertise (if applicable) is the liaison with any contractor(s). The museum is strongly committed to working with their external community either as team members with expertise or advocates for their programs.

## Budget and Financing Projects

The director in consultation with team members, a grant writer, and other advisors usually develops the budget for Shiloh's projects. Funding for projects is largely supplied via the museum's annual operating budget and is always assured in advance of startup. The museum does seek grant funds and individual contributions to support the projects, but there is not a formal development office at the museum. For large projects such as a facilities upgrade, the director and board president will be responsible for leading that function.

## Communications and Team Dynamics

As a small museum, Shiloh keeps meetings to a minimum, using email or informal discussions among staff and board as needed. Weekly staff meetings are a great opportunity to share updates on projects, as well as the monthly board meetings and regular City department head meetings. Communications with the community is important and done via social media and other web-based approaches. Lord has had much experience in working with all types of teams in her career and notes that size is not necessarily the most important factor for success; rather, it's having the skill sets needed for the type of project and effective working relationships. She notes: "Team members need not be tightly engaged, be in constant communication, or even like each other in order to perform well. But their dedication, skills, and mutual accountability must mesh or at least be articulated and effectively channeled by the project director." Like many others interviewed for this text, she feels that "trust and belief in each team member's work and commitment to the project" will lead to success. In regard to team conflict, she feels strongly that communications and oversight by the project director is critical. However, if conflict arises the issue should be addressed quickly. When the issues cannot be resolved due to personality conflict or lack of commitment and accountability, there would need to be a change in the membership of the team. Some of the team accountability issues that might occur include when team members do not have the skills needed for their assignments, or they cannot meet deadlines, or they may face an external problem or roadblock that is not promptly dealt with.

Shiloh is flexible in responding to setbacks, such as loss of a team member or changes in scope for a project, as long as they can make timely decisions, adjustments to timelines, or seek alternative funding.

*In Retrospect*

The museum undertakes a variety of project evaluation techniques, including internal review by staff and board, postproject team discussions, and external formal audience evaluations and views of stakeholders. These are useful for planning future work. The important factors regarding the implementation of projects relate to staff gaining expertise that can be done by observation as a team member or through professional development workshops. Lord's view of effective project management professionals includes the following skills:

- personnel management, understanding of group dynamics, and group facilitation

- budget management and fiscal responsibility

- identification and understanding of clear goal(s) and outcomes

- development and use of tools (e.g., Gantt charts, evaluations, visioning exercises)

- flexibility, the ability to multitask, and a willingness to seek assistance

- dedication and commitment to the project and its outcomes

- keeping one's eye on the big picture

- expertise in the area(s) needed for project success

Allyn Lord has spent thirty-four years in northwest Arkansas museums, including the University of Arkansas Museum and the Rogers Historical Museum. She has authored several history and museum books, serves as a peer reviewer for AAM and IMLS, and has been active in numerous professional museum organizations in Arkansas, the Southeast, and the United States. In her current role since 2005, Allyn has led the museum board and staff through a mission statement revision, three rounds of strategic planning, board restructuring, and new logo development while receiving more than $263,000 in grants and growing the museum's endowment by 152 percent. Allyn believes in the power of professional service and is particularly fond of working with and for small and mid-sized museums nationwide. She has recently been awarded lifetime achievement awards by the Arkansas Museums Association and the Southeastern Museums Conference.

### Michigan Museums Association

The Michigan Museums Association (MMA) is an organization dedicated to using project management techniques. Their executive director, Lisa Craig Brisson, applies project management in working with her board in developing and implementing the priority programs of the MMA and on their strategic planning. Brisson participated in the AASLH Project Management Workshop and became a strong advocate. As executive director and a staff of one, she needs to work closely with her board and to enlist the help of members in implementing their programs. MMA is an excellent example of how project management can make a huge difference in the success of operations of a small organization. As many of our museums are small, the MMA formula is a good model.[12]

MMA's board planning and decision making and its team process for programs closely follow the model of project management outlined in chapter 6. Brisson herself had been on the board and was keenly aware of the need most boards have to streamline their operations and at the same time achieve alignment behind their goals and objectives. Strategic planning is critical to assuring organizational sustainability. Brisson and her board consider a variety of program goals, and in deciding on priorities they look at several factors. The framework for decision making and implementation is illustrated in figure 10.1. Here is where the stages of project management enable the MMA to manage their work. Their life cycle mirrors that of most projects running through the steps of define, plan, execute, and finally evaluate. This is a great way to show the major activities in a project management process.

Brisson has created a template that serves as a charter outlining all the key assumptions and deliverables for projects. These include a project summary, objectives, risk assessment, requirements, constraints, and major milestones. Since implementing this new approach, the MMA board now makes substantive decisions about the definition of the project, is involved in the planning and execution only when the work involves something not in the charter and evaluates their outcome, and eliminates

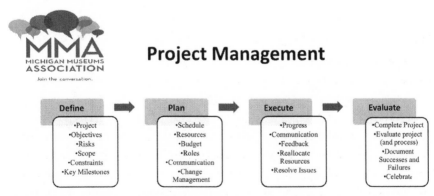

**Figure 10.1. Project management model. Courtesy of the Michigan Museums Association.**

any desire to micromanage or take on project work themselves. One of the key factors is to assign a board member as a "proxy" or board liaison to the project team. With a good deal of experience under their belt, the board is enthusiastic about this system. The expectations and flow of the process have been integrated so well with the work of the board and the operations of the organization that it has now become a core part of planning. Instead of creating an exhaustive strategic plan that includes detailed objectives and multiple action steps, the board now develops a strategic "framework" that indicates projects for each year with the beginning of the project definitions. Brisson says, "The use of project management with the board has resulted in a increased sense of trust in both directions. I can trust decisions made by the board about a project, and they can trust that they will have foundational input in all we do. It has created a very strong inter-board relationship, as well as a stronger board-director relationship."

The second way that MMA uses project management is creating teams to implement projects. Teams are formed from association members who work on projects such as the annual meeting, the workshop series, advocacy day, and fund-raising appeals. For example, for the annual conference as many as six teams are working on various activities including programs, events, awards and scholarships, revenue (sponsorships), on-site support (volunteers, setup), and communications. Each team has a task list and map of milestone dates as well as a leader appointed by Brisson. Members of the team are volunteers and eagerly seek the opportunity to build leadership skills as well as network with colleagues. Brisson has the teams working with Basecamp 3 project management software to monitor progress and share information among its membership.

With a formal degree in Museum Studies, Brisson has worked as an educator in a variety of history museums, as staff of the Visitor Studies Association, and a consultant on humanities and science education and interpretation projects. For those organizations thinking about implementing project management, Brisson suggests that starting small with an easy project will ease the organization into a new and more productive way of doing business. Like any change management program, this is wise advice.

## Conclusions

The case studies in this chapter reflect some common elements of best practices, including chartering, scheduling, and team planning and implementation. Each museum uses its own variation on the project management methodology. Another common practice is assigning a project sponsor or champion at a high level of the museum. In some museums that is the executive director; in others it may be a senior staff member or even a board member. The experiences described here also highlight the consistent need for adjustments and monitoring by a project manager. In addition, another common finding is that staff who manage projects have considerable knowledge of their field and the operations of the varied functions represented in the museum. The need to prepare the next generation of project professionals in the museum is clear. With models such as those in the case studies presented here along with the ongoing training programs and other resources outlined in this text, this much needed discipline will be applied widely in the field.

## Notes

1. Website accessed January 2, 2017, at http://cosi.org/about-cosi.

2. This case study is based on author interviews with Josh Sarver, Senior Director of Experiences, COSI, in November 2016 and January 2017.

3. This case study is based on author interviews with Cathy Frankel on October 24, 2016.

4. Website accessed on January 15, 2017, at http://creeculturalinstitute.ca.

5. Case study material provided from interviews by the author with Laura Phillips, November 2016 to January 2017.

6. Museum of Flight website, accessed December 27, 2016, at http://www.museumofflight.org.

7. Case material provided from interviews by the author with Rick Hardin, Project Manager, Museum of Flight, December 14, 2016.

8. The case study was developed from telephone and email informational interviews and documents provided to the author by staff who worked on this project—Peggy Day, Director of Strategic Projects; Elaine Harkins, former Facilities Director; and Kelly Tomajko, Director of Collections Operations—October 2016 to January 2017.

9. The information and illustrations in this case study was provided to the

author in email and telephone interviews by CEO Cinnamon Catlin-Legutko, January 3–5, 2017.

10. See Chapter 7 for discussion of Lencioni's theories on team dynamics.

11. Information and illustrations in this case study were provided to the author in email and telephone interviews by the director, Allyn Lord, December 2016–January 2017.

12. Information and illustrations provided to the author in email and telephone exchanges by Executive Director Lisa Craig Brisson, November 2016–January 2017.

# APPENDIX A

## EXHIBIT PLAN TEMPLATE

1. *Exhibit Title*—anticipated title of the exhibit.
2. *Project Manager*—museum staff member selected to manage the exhibit and author the plan. This individual is responsible for management of the exhibit plan, installation, and evaluation.
3. *Project Team Members*—museum staff members, contractors, advisors, and volunteers serving on the exhibit development team.
4. *Location*—exact location of where the exhibit will be installed.
5. *Overview*—this is a general statement summarizing the educational goals of the exhibit.
6. *Thesis Statement*—a brief statement or statements that define the exhibit's content area.
7. *Strategic Goal(s)*—a broad restating of the museum's strategic goal(s) that align with the exhibit's content.
8. *Educational Goal(s)*—the specific desired educational outcomes for the exhibit, which are ideally aligned with an OBE logic model.
9. *Stakeholders*—individuals who may be able to inform the development of the exhibit—tribal representatives, educators, anthropologists—and may be connected to the process through advisory committee meetings or other feedback channels.
10. *Funding Information*—identification of where the funding will come from and, if there isn't a known source, then a suggestion of possible funders.
11. *Audience*—the intended audience(s) for the exhibit—children, school groups, families, adults, and others.

12. *Boundaries*—other projects that will impact this exhibit and vice versa.

13. *Milestones*—steps along the way that will indicate the exhibit's progress and success.

14. *Deadline and Responsibilities*—specific dates by which work is to be presented, phased, completed, and more. Deadlines must be met when set to ensure success; therefore, dates should be carefully set, and be sure to take into consideration boundaries and other influencing factors. Museum staff members responsible for key deadlines and tasks need to be identified here.

**Table A.1.**

| Task | Responsibility | Due Date |
|------|----------------|----------|
|  |  |  |
|  |  |  |
|  |  |  |
|  |  |  |
|  |  |  |
|  |  |  |
|  |  |  |
|  |  |  |
|  |  |  |

15. *Budget*—an itemization of the costs associated with this exhibit, including dedicated staff hours.

16. *Documentation*—attach to the plan any previous planning documentation that adds to the success of the exhibit; for example, exhibit schematic, bibliography, and more.

**Table A.2.**

| Item | Purpose | Quantity | Cost | Total |
|------|---------|----------|------|-------|
|      |         |          |      |       |
|      |         |          |      |       |
|      |         |          |      |       |
|      |         |          |      |       |
|      |         |          |      |       |
|      |         |          |      |       |
|      |         |          |      |       |
|      |         |          |      |       |
|      |         |          |      |       |

Courtesy Abbe Museum.

# APPENDIX B

## Exhibit Postmortem Results

Exhibit Name:
Participants:

**Table B.1.**

|  | What went well | What didn't go well | Takeaway ideas and opportunities |
|---|---|---|---|
| **Overall Concept**<br>Defining and refining goals and ideas<br>Content<br>Objects and images<br>Graphics, style, and layout<br>Press<br>Opening<br>Evaluation<br>Team dynamics |  |  |  |
| **Content**<br>Travel<br>Interviews<br>Editing process<br>Team dynamics and decision-making process<br>Research<br>Presentation of content |  |  |  |
| **Collections**<br>Object selection process<br>Image selection<br>Loan process<br>Layout and presentation of objects |  |  |  |

| | | | |
|---|---|---|---|
| **Graphics**<br>Style sheet<br>Layout<br>Sketch up<br>Panels<br>Printing<br>Mounting | | | |
| **Fabrication**<br>Budget<br>Hiring<br>In-house<br>Contractors | | | |
| **Installation**<br>Objects<br>Images<br>Panels | | | |
| **PR**<br>Invitation/postcard<br>Press coverage<br>Web coverage | | | |
| **Other** | | | |

Courtesy Abbe Museum.

# APPENDIX C

## Committee Charter Template

### Abbe Museum

It is strongly suggested that each committee develop a charter. This will direct the responsibilities and goals of each committee.

Committee charters will:

- prevent project overlap;

- prevent overarching authority;

- promote consistency;

- create positive energy;

- illuminate what type of work is involved, which helps when appointing committee members;

- enable a committee to manage project/committee budgets better.

## Definitions:

*Charter*—a charter is a written road map that defines the key questions or issues to be addressed by the committee as well as any high-level deliverables. It may also include information such as committee composition or the relationship of the committee to the organization's strategic or operational goals. But if it does nothing else, a committee charter should include, with a reasonable degree of detail, a committee's purpose and its intended outcomes.

In addition to a description of the committee, the charter also serves to establish the committee's (and the chair's) authorities. For this reason, board members should pay attention to charters to ensure that reasonable committee parameters are established. Chairpersons should be certain that the charter provides them with sufficient authorities and resources to accomplish the stated committee objectives.

It is strongly suggested that committee charters be publicized and widely disseminated among interested parties. They should not be kept secret, and they should be thoroughly vetted with board members and other interested stakeholders before the resulting committee gets underway.

*Deliverables*—a tangible outcome to a committee's work, usually contingent upon a specified period of time; for example, annual budget, historic preservation project, educational program, and more.

## Elements:

Each charter should be written around these elements. Portions of the bylaws can be inserted when needed. An explanation of each element is below.

*Committee Overview*—this is a general statement summing the purpose, goals, and resources (committee members are resources) involved.

*Scope*—a brief statement or statements that define the committee's area of influence and the areas it does not have influence over. Authority may be defined here.

*Objectives*—a point-by-point listing of the committee's objectives and responsibilities. Management of responsibilities may be defined here.

*Strategic Goals*—a broad restating of the museum's strategic goals; illustrates committee's alignment with the broader strategic plan.

*Measures/Deliverables*—How will you know the committee has followed the charter or mission? Measures include: certification or accreditation.

Deliverables include: a viable endowment, capital improvements, a specific plan of action, and more.

*Budget/Funding Information*—If the committee's success required financial support, where will the money come from?

*Customers*—Who will benefit from the committee? The general public, the board, general membership, the staff, others?

*Boundaries*—What other committees or projects will impact this committee, and vice versa?

*Milestones*—steps along the way that indicate the committee's progress and success.

*Deadlines*—firm, specific dates by which work is to be presented, projects completed, and more. Deadlines must be met when set to ensure success; therefore, dates should be carefully set and take into consideration boundaries and other influencing factors.

*Supporting Documentation*—attach to the charter any previous planning documentation that adds to the charter; for example, bylaws, excerpts, project specifications, and more.

## Charter Management:

When completed, each charter will be approved by all pertinent committee members and presented at the next board meeting for approval (the organization could also decide that committee approval is sufficient).

If there are any changes in the charter, an addendum will be attached to the original charter. A charter is only figuratively set in stone.

All charters and any addendums will be kept in a central location for board members, staff, and general membership (if applicable).

All charters should be approved no later than a specified board meeting date. Committees should work on their charter during their first meeting.

Charters should be reviewed and possibly revised every three (3) years, or as needed.

# APPENDIX D

## Accountability Chart

| Phase | Product | Component | Responsibility |
|---|---|---|---|
| **Idea** | Stakeholder Analysis | | Leadership Team/ Sponsor |
| | | | |
| **Preconcept** | Research Papers | | Project Sponsor |
| | | Industry Review | Project Sponsor |
| | | Literature Review | Project Sponsor |
| | | Front-End Evaluation Report | Sr. Director of Evaluation |
| | Logic Model | | Project Sponsor |
| | Preconcept Narrative | | Project Sponsor |
| | | Project Description | Project Sponsor |
| | | Project Budget (Estimate) | Senior Director Experience Design and Production |
| | | Project Schedule (Estimate) | Senior Director Experience Design and Production |
| | | | |
| **Development** | Source for Funding | | Leadership Team/ Sponsor |
| | | | |
| **Administrative** | Statement of Work | | Leadership Team/ Sponsor |
| | Project Charter | | Project Sponsor |
| | Detailed ProjectSchedule (WBS) | | Project Manager |
| | Project Reports | | Project Manager |

| Phase | Product | Component | Responsibility |
|---|---|---|---|
| **Concept** | Concept Narrative | | Project Manager |
| | | Experience Theme | Project Manager |
| | | Project Budget Spreadsheet (Estimate) | Project Manager |
| | | Component Briefs | Associate Producer |
| | | Sketch Drawings | Exhibit Designer |
| **Design** | Design Narrative | | Project Manager |
| | | Component Budget Spreadsheet (Final) | Associate Producer |
| | | Element Briefs | Associate Producer |
| | | Prototypes | Fabricator |
| | | Detailed Drawings | Exhibit Designer |
| | Formative Evaluations | | Project Evaluator |
| **Fabrication** | Exhibition Completion | | Project Manager |
| | Component Completion | | Associate Producer |
| | | Exhibit Fabrication | Fabricator |
| | | Operations Manual | Associate Producer |
| | | Programs Manual | Associate Producer |
| | Remedial Evaluation | | Project Evaluator |
| | Remedial Budget | | Project Manager |
| | Remedial Completion | | Associate Producer |
| | | Remedial Fabrication | Fabricator |
| **Implementation** | Implementation Narrative | | Project Manager |

| | | Operations Document | Project Manager |
|---|---|---|---|
| | | Operations/ Maintenance Budget | Associate Producer |
| | Training | | Associate Producer |
| **Closure** | Project Closure | | Project Sponsor |
| | | Evaluation Report | Sr. Director of Evaluation |
| | | Closure Celebration | Project Manager |
| | | Project Documentation | Project Manager |

Courtesy COSI.

# APPENDIX E

## Exhibit Project Charter

**Sample Charter**

DATE:
TO:        Project Director
FROM:      John L. Gray  ★
SUBJECT:   Charter for Exhibition

1. **Project:**
2. **Opening Date:**
3. **Location:**
4. **Description of Key Message(s):**
5. **Project Team Members:**
     *Project Director:*
     *Curator:*
     *Project Manager:*
     *Collections Manager:*
     *Designer:*
     *Interpretive Planner:*
6. **Budget:**
7. **Schedule/Deliverables:**
     Design:
     Review:
     Production Handshake:
     Installation:

# APPENDIX F

## Project Proposal Form

**Table F.1.  Nebraska State Historical Society Project Proposal Form**

| Proposed Project Name: | |
|---|---|
| Submitted by: | Date: |
| Project Objectives (*the objectives should be concisely written so they can be evaluated after the completion of the project to see whether they were achieved. The objectives should be specific and measurable*): | |
| What opportunity will this realize for NSHS? (*Or what problem will it solve?*): | |
| Project Deliverables (*What will the project include when completed?*): | |
| How will you measure the success of this project? (*What evaluation techniques will you use?*): | |
| Assumptions (*What resources will be available, whose help do you need, and what commitments do you assume will be made to the project?*): | |
| Constraints and Risks (*What could derail this project? What are the most likely reasons for failure?*): | |
| Budget (rough budget and potential funding sources): | |
| Draft Schedule (*When will the project begin and end? List major milestones if known.*): | |
| Potential Team Members for this project: | |

**Table F.1. (Continued)**

| Additional Comments or Information: | |
|---|---|
| Project Approval Date: | Project Manager Assigned: |
| Approved by: | Signature: |

When developing your proposal, please remember that all projects *must*:

1. be strongly tied to at least one (and preferably multiple) strategic plan goals.
2. have clearly defined measurable objectives.
3. evaluate success on how these objectives are met.
4. build on or support the work of other teams.
5. provide a positive return on our investment.

In addition, NSHS projects are *strongly encouraged* to:

1. communicate NSHS's value and values.
2. showcase what NSHS has to offer and cross-sell other programs or opportunities.
3. encourage membership in NSHS.

Courtesy Nebraska State Historical Society.

# APPENDIX G

## Hypothetical Project Planning Exercise

The Midwest Museum of Unusual Stuff is considering an exhibition on "Dogs in the White House." A local collector, Ima Hound, has amassed over fifty artifacts, including oil paintings, cartoons, photographs, dog toys and collars, rare LBJ dog ears, and presidential dog face masks that are made of varying materials from wood to cardboard to sequined coconut shells. The latter were worn by the collector to a variety of Halloween parties that preceded the November elections for the past three decades.

On September 1 the board chair of MMUS asks the director to do everything possible to open this exhibition on October 30 in time for Halloween.

The museum has the following staff members:

Director
    Administrator
    Curator of Unusual Objects
    Librarian/Archivist
    Registrar
    Educator
    Docent Coordinator
    Exhibition Curator/Designer
    Facilities Manager
    Development Officer

The changing gallery space is currently hosting a traveling exhibition that closes October 25.

The "Dogs in the White House" exhibition will require the following activities: loan negotiation, conservation review and treatment, exhibition design and production and installation, fund-raising, marketing, docent training, and preparing the gallery space with new walls.

## YOUR TASK:

1. Decide who on the staff needs to be on the project team (core and extended).
2. Suggest a timeline for opening the exhibition.
3. Note what activities need to occur in what order.

What might go wrong?

Courtesy of the Author.

# APPENDIX H

## Hypothetical Team Planning Exercise

The River City Science Museum recently received a major cash pledge from a pharmaceutical corporation to underwrite an exhibition on Health in America. The curator, Jack Malady, at the request of the director, Mary Sureright, worked closely with the exhibits designer to develop a scope, timeline, budget, and script.

About three months before the show was to open, Malady presented the exhibit plan to the director, who promptly turned it over to the registrar, conservator, the educator, and the museum's development office for comments. The first person to respond was the registrar, who told the director that he has two major outgoing loans, a large year-end gift to process, and a pending collections move and can't process the loans for the Health exhibition without hiring additional help. He also said, "The morale around here is really low. This exhibit is going to kill us!" The conservator reminded everyone how busy she is and then said, "At least 30 percent of the objects you selected for this show need extensive work." The educator said, "Let's do something daring . . . let's ask the public to vote on which artifacts they would like to see in this exhibition! It will only take a few weeks to gather that information."

Budget: The director asked for estimates from an outside production firm, but due to incredible demand for new blockbuster exhibitions in the museums in River City they were short staffed. They could do the Health exhibition job in three months, but the cost would be higher than normal. Malady's budget tripled. The development director looked at the budget and said, "This is way over what our funder has pledged." "And, oh by the way, the money isn't coming in 'til next year."

Sureright was gathering all this information for a senior staff meeting when she received an urgent phone call from board chair Roger Rant. He was concerned about articles he was reading regarding the funding of exhibitions at the Smithsonian. He said, "It's something to do with accepting money from a sponsor who is in the same business as your exhibition topic. I hope we never do that!"

At the meeting with her senior staff Sureright says, "We got trouble at River City!" She outlines all the facts and then says, "What are we going to do about this mess?" In your groups, please review the situation and consider how the River City Science Museum can handle this problem. Consider the fundamentals of project management, decision making, employee morale, and museum ethics.

What process should have been used to produce a credible budget and realistic schedule?

Who needs to be involved in the decision making for an exhibition? How will the museum obtain the additional funding or resources? Is cash flow a concern?

Will changes be needed involving collections or the production schedule? If the opening date has to change, how will the museum deal with the public reaction?

What steps need to be taken to deal with staff morale given this situation?

How does the museum deal with the outside funder given the board chair's concerns? Is there an ethical concern here? New policies needed?

River City organizational units include:

Curatorial
  Visitor Experience
  Development/Public Relations
  Registrar
  Conservation
  Administration
  Technology

Courtesy of the Author.

# SELECTED BIBLIOGRAPHY

Ackerson, Anne W., and Joan H. Baldwin. *Leadership Matters*. Lanham, MD: AltaMira Press, 2014.

Adizes, Ichak. *Managing Corporate Lifecycles*. Paramus: Prentice Hall, 1999.

Anderson, Gail. *Museum Mission Statements: Building a Distinct Identity*. Washington, DC: American Association of Museums, 1998.

Baker, Sunny, and Kim Baker. *On Time/On Budget*. Paramus: Prentice Hall, 1992.

Bergeron, Anne, and Beth Tuttle. *Magnetic: The Art and Science of Engagement*. Washington DC: American Association of Museums Press, 2013.

Bolman, Lee G., and Terrence E. Deal. *Reframing Organizations*. New York: John Wiley, 2008.

Carpenter, Julie. *Project Management in Libraries, Archives and Museums: Working with Government and Other External Partners*. London: Elsevier, 2010.

Chew, Ron. "Forum: Toward a More Agile Model of Exhibition Making." *Museum News* 79 (2000): 6.

Collins, James C. *Good to Great*. New York: HarperBusiness, 2001.

———. *Good to Great and the Social Sectors: Why Business Thinking Is Not the Answer*. New York: HarperBusiness, 2005.

Crimm, Walter, Martha Morris, and L. Carole Wharton. *Planning Successful Museum Building Projects*. Lanham, MD: AltaMira Press, 2009.

Davies, Maurice, and Lucy Shaw. "Diversifying the Museum Workforce: The Diversify Scheme and Its Impact on Participants' Careers." *Museum Management and Curatorship* 28, no. 2 (2013): 172–92.

Dean, David K. "Planning for Success: Project Management for Museum Exhibitions." In *International Handbooks of Museum Studies* (Hoboken: John Wiley & Sons), 2015. Published online at http://onlinelibrary.wiley.com/doi/10.1002/9781118829059.wbihms216/full.

Drucker, Peter. *Managing the Nonprofit Organization*. New York: HarperCollins, 1990.

Edmondson, Amy. *Teaming: How Organizations Learn, Innovate, and Compete in the Knowledge Economy*. San Francisco: Jossey-Bass, 2012.

Falk, John, and Beverly Sheppard. *Thriving in the Knowledge Age*. Lanham, MD: AltaMira Press, 2006.

Faron, Rich et al. "Exhibitors at the Crossroads: Building Better Museum Teams." *Exhibitionist* 24, no. 2 (2005): 44–48.

Faron, Rich, and Susan Curran. "Team Building: Thoughts on Working Well with Others." *Exhibitionist* 26, no. 2 (2007): 32–38.

Fisher, Roger, and William Ury. *Getting to Yes*. New York: Penguin Books, 1991.

Frame, J. Davidson. *Managing Projects in Organizations*. San Francisco: Jossey-Bass, 2003.

Genoways, Hugh, Lynne M. Ireland, and Cinnamon Catlin-Legutko. *Museum Administration 2.0*. Lanham, MD: Rowman & Littlefield, 2017.

Gurian, Elaine Heumann. *Institutional Trauma*. Washington, DC: American Association of Museums, 1995.

Heifetz, Ronald, and Donald Laurie. *The Practice of Adaptive Leadership*. Boston: Harvard Business Press, 2009.

Hersey, Paul, Kenneth H. Blanchard, and Dewey E. Johnson. *Management of Organizational Behavior*, 10th ed. Gambrills, MD: Pearson, 2013.

Janes, Robert. *Museums and the Paradox of Change*. Calgary: Glenbow Museum and the University of Calgary Press, 1997.

Katzenbach, Jon R., and Douglas K. Smith. *The Wisdom of Teams*. New York: HarperCollins, 2003.

Kayser, Thomas A. *Mining Group Gold*. El Segundo: Serif Publishing, 1990.

Keene, Suzanne. *Managing Conservation in Museums*. London: Routledge, 2002.

Knowles, Loraine. "Project Management in Practice: The Museum of Liverpool Life." In *Management in Museums*, edited by Kevin Moore, 113–48. London: Althone Press, 1999.

La Piana, David. *The Nonprofit Strategy Revolution*. New York: Fieldstone Alliance, 2008.

Lee, Charlotte P. "Reconsidering Conflict in Exhibition Development Teams." *Museum Management and Curatorship* 22, no. 2 (2007): 183–99.

Lencioni, Patrick. *The Five Dysfunctions of a Team*. San Francisco: Jossey-Bass, 2002.

Lewis, James P. *Team-Based Project Management*. New York: American Management Association, 1998.

Lord, Barry, and Maria Piacente. *Manual of Museum Exhibitions*. Lanham, MD: Rowman & Littlefield, 2014.

Lord, Gail Dexter, and Barry Lord. *The Manual of Museum Management*. Lanham, MD: AltaMira Press, 2009.

Lord, Gail Dexter, Barry Lord, and Lindsay Martin. *The Manual of Museum Planning*. Lanham, MD: AltaMira Press, 2012.

Lord, Gail Dexter, and Kate Markert. *The Manual of Strategic Planning for Museums*. Lanham, MD: AltaMira Press, 2007.

McKenna-Cress, Polly, and Janet Kamien. *Creating Exhibitions*. New York: John Wiley and Sons, 2013.

Merritt, Elizabeth, and Victoria Garvin. *Secrets of Institutional Planning*. Washington, DC: American Association of Museums, 2007.

Morris, Martha. "Recent Trends in Exhibition Development." *Exhibitionist* 21, no. 1 (2002): 8–12.

———. "Staff Development and Training at the National Museum of American History." *ICOM Study Series* 10 (2002): 19–20.

———. "Vision, Values, Voice: The Leadership Challenge." In *Museum Studies*, edited by Stephen Williams and Catharine A. Hawks, 35–46. Society for the Preservation of Natural History Collections, 2006.

Myerson, Debra. *Tempered Radicals: How Everyday Leaders Inspire Change at Work*. Cambridge: Harvard Business School Press, 2003.

Norris, Linda, and Rainey Tisdale. *Creativity in Museum Practice*. Walnut Creek, CA: Left Coast Press, 2014.

Patterson, K., J. Grenny, R. McMillan, and A. Switzler. *Crucial Conversations: Tools for Talking When Stakes Are High*. New York: McGraw-Hill, 2002.

Rounds, Jay, and Nancy McIlvaney. "Who's Using the Team Process? How's It Going?" *Exhibitionist* 19, no. 1 (2000): 3–15.

Senge, Peter. *The Fifth Discipline: The Art & Practice of the Learning Organization*. New York: Doubleday, 1990.

Zimmerman, Steve, and Jeanne Bell. *The Sustainability Mindset: Using the Matrix Map to Make Strategic Decisions*. San Francisco: Jossey-Bass, 2015.

# INDEX

*Note: Illustrations are in italics*

# ABOUT THE AUTHOR

**Martha Morris** is associate professor emeritus at the George Washington University in Washington, D.C. She has over forty-five years of experience in the museum field as a manager and leader. Her career began in registration and collections management at the Corcoran Gallery of Art and later at the Smithsonian's National Museum of American History, where she eventually served as deputy director. Her work and her teaching have consistently focused on management practices, including strategic planning, project management, teambuilding, staff development, and facilities projects. As a member of the board of the Midatlantic Association of Museums, she served as founding program chair of the Building Museums symposium. She has designed workshops and lectured and written on a number of topics, including collections planning and management, exhibition development, staffing, museum facilities programs, museum mergers, and twenty-first-century leadership skills. She holds BA and MA degrees in art history and a masters in business administration.

Made in the USA
Lexington, KY
11 August 2017